Growing Up Catholic

John Walsh was born and brought up in South London
and educated by the Jesuits of Wimbledon College
and at the universities of Oxford and Dublin.
He is now Literary Editor of *The Sunday Times*.

Growing Up
Catholic

John Walsh

Illustrations by Marie-Hélène Jeeves

PAPERMAC

First published 1989 by
PAPERMAC
a division of Macmillan Publishers Limited
4 Little Essex Street London WC2R 3LF
and Basingstoke

Associated companies in Auckland, Delhi, Dublin, Gaborone,
Hamburg, Harare, Hong Kong, Johannesburg, Kuala Lumpur,
Lagos, Manzini, Melbourne, Mexico City, Nairobi, New York,
Singapore and Tokyo

ISBN 0-333-45738-2

A CIP catalogue record for this book is available from the British
Library.

Typeset by Wyvern Typesetting Ltd, Bristol
Printed in Great Britain
by Richard Clay Ltd,
Bungay, Suffolk

This book is dedicated to my parents:

Anne Walsh, who taught me respect and veneration, and the late Martin Walsh, who taught me you could laugh at them both – with love and apologies for the ensuing libels.

Contents

Acknowledgments   ix
Preface   xi

1 Gentle Jesus: Early Catholicism   1
2 Sin, Vice, Hell and Eternity   11
3 Going to Church   34
4 Education   50
5 Catholic Sex   73
6 The Catholic Personnel Department   96
7 The Sacraments   115
8 The Catholic Hardware Department   129
9 The Catholic Community   139

Epilogue: Going Off The Idea   158

Acknowledgments

MY THANKS are due to the scores of Catholics, lapsed or otherwise, to whom I talked during the planning and writing of this book: especially to Harry Armfield, George Bull, Madelyn Brody, Wendy Perriam, Karen Armstrong, Jo Foley, Maggie Pringle, Rebecca Fraser, Clare Toynbee, Beryl Bainbridge and Peter Barnes.

I am grateful to Robert Nowell for alerting me to the wonders of the Baltimore Catechism; to Kate Jones, my strict but supportive editor at Macmillan; to Kyle Cathie, for initiating this enjoyable project; and to Carolyn and Sophie for providing many welcome distractions from it.

Credits

THE AUTHOR would like to thank the following for their kind permission to reprint extracts: The Catholic Truth Society for *A Catechism of Christian Doctrine*; William Collins Sons & Co. Ltd for *Why I am Still a Catholic* edited by Robert Nowell; Hamish Hamilton for *The Stories of Frank O'Connor* by Frank O'Connor; William Heinemann Ltd for *Little Wilson and Big God* by Anthony Burgess; Martin Secker & Warburg Ltd for *How Far Can You Go?* by David Lodge; The Society of Authors as the literary representative of the Estate of James Joyce. The publishers have made every effort to trace copyright holders. If we have inadvertently omitted to acknowledge anyone we should be most grateful if this could be brought to our attention for correction.

Preface

TO BEGIN as all good sermons begin . . . The other day, as I was having a drink in Covent Garden with a friend, we were both accosted by a not-especially decrepit beggar. 'Could ye ever,' he asked, 'spare thirty pence for the bus?'

Accustomed to having one's conversation thus interrupted in the heart of London, I went on talking but abstractedly dug around in my pockets for some silver. I came up with exactly seven pence. 'Paul,' I said, 'this is no good. Have you got any change?' Surprised that the beggar should suddenly take on such importance, Paul investigated his own pockets and produced precisely three pence. I looked with sudden horror at the paltry alms lying in my hand, wondered if I should change a fiver at the bar, decided not and proffered it anyway. 'I'm terribly sorry,' I said to the beggar's retreating form, 'I'm afraid the rest went on the fag machine . . .'

'For God's sake,' said Paul. 'Do you have to be so bloody *Catholic* about it?'

He was right. It was a classic Sin of Omission, in which another human soul, who might well have been Christ or one of his wilier angels acting incognito, has asked to be fed, watered, clothed or sheltered, and I had failed him. To Paul it was a ridiculous act to apologise to a beggar for not coming up to scratch. To me too, a moment later, it was something to be laughed off. But for those brief seconds I had – almost unconsciously – reverted back to a world where one was constantly on the lookout for signs of virtue and vice, of good works and sins, of Purgatorial souls in need of assistance and of Heavenly icons to pray to for one's own salvation and redemption from the jaws of Hell: the world of the active Catholic.

You can meet Catholics in any walk of life and think them the most ordinary of people. They can be ordinary factory workers, ordinary bankers and civil servants, ordinary sportsmen and soldiers, even (*mutatis mutandis*) ordinary Cabinet Ministers. Some may still attend Mass every day. Some may not have been near the sacraments of Confession and Communion for many years. But for all of us, a memory still abides: the huge, unrepeatable, unforgettable series of images that filled the heart, mind and soul as we went through the experience of a Catholic childhood.

The pages that follow are an attempt to describe that awesome process, from the first nursery promptings about God and the Devil to the final adolescent arguments that preceded one's departure from the congregation of the faithful. What follows may appear sardonic, even – to some – blasphemous. All I mean to do is to represent, as faithfully as possible, the impressions that were stamped on my imagination, by the combined forces of parents, teachers, priests, nuns, catechisms, statues, holy books and the various gleanings of school gossip, of the world that supposedly lay before us: a world which, reduced to its simplest formulation, meant that by your own behaviour, whether public or private, well-meant or dreadfully deliberate, conscious or unconscious, you were steering your poor uncomprehending self into utter perdition day after day.

It's a book that I wish I had had near to hand when I was young. Today things no longer stand as they once did. The Catholic Church has changed since the fifties and sixties when I was growing up. Several stories we were told at school will not be told to the eighties or nineties generation of Papist tots. Many details of Church services, of the smartly edited new catechism, of the daily ritual of the secular Catholic, of the rumours and threats and institutionalised misinformation of school, of the whole angry buzz of sin and doctrine and prayer, will (especially since the Second Vatican Council) have been withdrawn in the intervening years, to be remembered like the echoes of a forgotten choir.

But enough remains in today's Catholic Church (or so I would argue) to make this exercise in wondering out loud relevant to a new generation. Because although the circumstances change, the message doesn't. Those who (in Anthony Burgess's fine phrase) 'had Hell injected in our veins at an impressionable age' remain an élite among the guilty and the repressed. We can never be free of its entry into the spiritual bloodstream. Our response to the outside world is still changed utterly by it.

Here you will read of the traumas of Confession and other sacraments; of the unworldly Catholic's notions of sex and nuns and miraculous medals, of three-hour ceremonials and jolly but implacable priests, of the sense of unfairness that accompanied one's parroted learning of the Catechism, of the unimaginable heights of Heaven and the ineradicable horrors of Hell. It has been for me a shriving and exorcism of youthful sins and demons. I hope the book may awake an answering chord in other Catholics, of whatever generation, and a wide-eyed fascination among those who never knew either the unexpected bliss or the unspeakable nightmare of growing up Catholic.

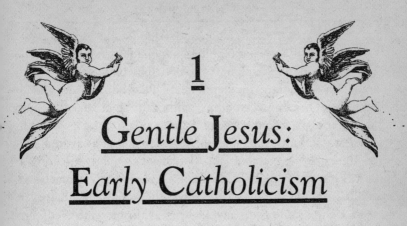

1

Gentle Jesus: Early Catholicism

I WAS SIX YEARS OLD when I saw the Devil in the street. I was walking back home with my mother from Sunday Benediction at St Vincent's in the next street. I was buttoned up warmly in my little green greatcoat, hands encased in mittens, legs in woolly grey socks and sensible junior brogues. We were going back for my favourite early supper of chipolata sausages and everything felt right with the world.

We turned the corner of Altenburg Gardens, where it meets the north side of Clapham Common in a blare of lights and traffic on the South Circular. I heard a car horn go Beep! and turned my head away from my mother's protective smile, and looked straight into the face of Satan.

He was absurdly tall, was passing barely a foot away from me on the narrow pavement, was (I remember clearly) wearing a pointy hat and a pointy beard like a self-consciously symmetrical goblin, and was smiling at me. It was the worst sight I had ever seen. He was smiling into my eyes with a horrible wide-eyed leer, because he knew that I was marked down for Hell and that whatever I did to improve myself throughout my whole life, he would be there at the end, waiting with the same repellent grin, at last able to announce that he was taking me away . . .

I turned to ice, from head to foot. The only parts of me left unfrozen by the spectacle were my lungs, and I screamed until I shook.

The poor man cannot have enjoyed the experience any more than I did. Before I was pulled home in a quivering semi-coma, I was heard gibbering about the Devil to my increasingly embarrassed mother; whether this tribute to his unlovely features was better or worse, from his point of view, than having the other Sunday evening passers-by assume he'd tried to attack a six-year-old child and his mother, was something I wondered about only later. The only thing of which he was guilty was in corresponding too well with the picture the average Catholic child builds up of the Final Enemy.

It's a far more vivid picture than any the child has of God. Ironically, the Supreme Being, the Maker of Heaven and Earth, the Creator and Redeemer of Mankind tends to take second place to the Devil in the mental iconography of the six-year-old. One cannot blame it on the parents or suggest they are trying to scare their tiny charges into submission. On the contrary. From the outset, Catholic parents fill their children's heads with talk of God: how He made you, how He loves you, how He's always around when you need Him, how you should always try to be like Him. As a result, God starts to be imagined as part of the snug, domestic, safe cocoon of home, reassuring and cosy. He is almost one of the family – a favourite uncle, say, or a slightly tottery grandfather you accept along with the furniture but pay no further heed to. Then into this charming domestic scene bursts the figure of Satan.

Out in the real world, people refer to the Devil in surprisingly light terms. The familiarity with which the secular hoi polloi regard the King of Darkness seems extraordinary. He is given jovial soubriquets like 'Old Nick' as though some benevolent old character on the local darts team. He's intellectualised into Mephistopheles, or blandified into some vaguely naughty but lovable imp in the popular imagination.

What a debasement of reputation for the figure who pervaded our imaginations. We were terrified of the Devil. We thought of him all the time. We knew he was out to get us, with his long fingernails and mad eyes. If he was too busy torturing small babies in some remote region of his empire actually to come for us *in person*, we knew a few battalions of his wicked angels – who would resemble school bullies, only taller, leaner and more spidery – were constantly on hand to deputise.

'That's the Devil talking,' someone would say, if you demanded to know why you couldn't have what you wanted. Great. So he was already inside you, commandeering your vocal chords like some malevolent ventriloquist. Did we believe it? Of course we did. A sudden, uncharacteristically violent fit of swearing, and you felt your nice everyday self had been taken over. To him we ascribed several of the attributes supposedly exclusive to God. He was everywhere. He knew our deepest secret thoughts, but unlike good old ineffectual God, he was always ready to play on them and use them for our destruction or capture. He was an organiser of rare talent – it was the Devil who convened gatherings of bad boys on missions to skip off school, assault tiny victims or chase girls and pull their hair. It was likewise he who invented public houses, brought rude films into local cinemas, started wars, invaded countries and brought public figures into disrepute.

─────────── ANTHONY BURGESS ───────────

I was now taught some Catholicism, which chiefly had to do with eternal punishment for trivial offences. We were told that each of us had a guardian angel, an invisible monitor even in the lavatory, and we sang a song to him or her or it:

> *Guardian angel, from Heaven so bright,*
> *Watching beside me to keep me aright.*
> *Fold thy wings round me and guard me with love*
> *Softly sing songs to me of heav'n above.*
> *Beautiful angel, so tender and mild,*
> *Lovingly guard me, for I am thy child.*

It was a harmless and charming fiction; it still is. But the Manichee in us all, even at the age of six, had to assume that there was another angel, a very bad one, hitting out at the pale epicene from Heaven, and, since fighting was a sin, winning most of the rounds.

(from *Little Wilson and Big God*, Penguin 1988)

─────────────────────────────

Once at primary school, my friend Andrew and I drew a picture of the Devil, as a fatuously cackling ringmaster with a top-hat, a whip, greased mustachios and bandy legs. We even gave him a silly wife to show our contempt for his domestic circumstances, a sort of portly Cruella de Ville who would nag and bully him without mercy. The reason for our little portrait escapes me but the underlying intention was clear: we were showing that he didn't frighten us, *oh* no, we didn't care a crumb about his sinister threats and sneaky arrangements for our perdition. We would be all right because we were good Catholic boys who loved God and were secure in his returned love. He could (how we sniggered) go to Hell . . .

But that was during the daytime. Andrew agreed that I could keep the picture, so I took it home and stuck it on my bedroom wall. Time passed. It grew dark. I had occasion to visit the room once or twice in the evening before bedtime, and each time the picture on the wall drew my eyes with ever more fearful foreboding. Away from my brave friend, surrounded by the lurking terrors of night, I began to feel I had done something dreadful.

Paranoia began to steal its way. Why had Andrew not taken the blasted thing? Was he scared as well? Did he realise that it was just asking for trouble? Was not the Devil, even at this moment, bridling with fury at being thus insulted? Was he summoning the most unpleasant emissary in his entourage and telling him to speed my doom, and bring me to Hell first thing in the morning? It was ghastly. How could I tell anyone that I'd been rude about Satan and was terrified of the consequences? Finally I took the only available course of action. With my eyes tight shut, I ripped the picture off the wall, tore it into a million bits and breathed a silent, placatory 'Sorry' to the unseen demon. The next day, rather than feel a fool about such behaviour, I assured myself it was only sensible to be on the safe side.

While Satan was singly and unchangingly horrible, God occupied a bafflingly varied number of incarnations. God the Father seemed to us a distant old cove, something between Santa Claus without the joviality and Old Father Time without the scythe. I thought of him as a crustily ancient sea-captain mumbling cantankerous words of advice to an audience of stroppy delinquents. He was all right for the grown-ups, we thought, with their peculiar indulgence towards valetudinarian bores and deaf old gits; but he wouldn't really like children at all.

Jesus Christ was presented to us in stages. In the Christmas crib, he was Baby Jesus, cooingly intelligent, surmounted by the golden dish of a halo, as he graciously accepted the veneration of the gaudily robed, swarthy Kings from foreign lands, and the presumably neutral attention of the local oxen. Of his precocious wisdom and innocent perfection we heard much. But we knew he was really only a doll, to be picked up and laid down by little girls as part of their soppy rituals.

The Boy Jesus, back-chatting his greybeard elders, ignoring his earthly father (surely the most unprepossessing and dimly imagined person in the Bible) and ticking off his mother when she questioned his authority, was a far more attractive rôle-model. When he graduated to tough manhood and kicked the stallholders and moneylenders out of the temple, he seemed an enviably direct operator, like a licensed hooligan with Right for ever on his side. All the chat we were fed about 'Gentle Jesus, meek and mild' seemed either misrepresentation or the wishful thinking of religion teachers. You felt he would have given them a hard time if they'd met.

When the Passion of Christ is first read to you, its effect is unbearably exciting. The story of capture and release and capture again, of shaky testimony and innocent betrayal (the pusillanimous St Peter especially comes across as a classic filmic stool-pigeon, played by Elisha Cook Jnr), the long catalogue of flogging, crowning with thorns, the slow drag through the streets under a cross to which he will finally be nailed . . . It adds up to a brutal iconography of moral confrontation that never leaves you.

I was awakened one night just before Easter when I was hardly older than four or five, and brought downstairs to watch a dramatisation of the Passion on TV (a rare treat – the only other such occasion I recall it happening was for the last appearance of the Crazy Gang). The black and white screen was filled with marching soldiers as they converged on Gethsemane. Judas was an easily recognisable ne'er-do-well with a black beard and nervously flickering eyes. The other Apostles were fleeing like schoolgirls. Jesus Christ was a pale, sad-eyed milksop who gave in with what seemed like spineless resignation to everything that Pilate and the Jewish mob threw at him.

I was profoundly upset by the ensuing barbarities, not because they were cruel or gratuitously awful, but because they rocked your conception of Christ as a rôle-model. Remembering that Christ stood above all else for the power of love, you felt let down that his power should fail so flatly at his most critical hour. Fed on Popeye, William Tell, Desperate Dan and the various swashbucklers who dominated TV in the late fifties, I was quite unused to the unrelieved tragedy of the Crucifixion. Was not this, I asked myself, sounding like some junior Pharisee, the man who cured the sick and brought people back from death? Could he not, I wondered like Pontius Pilate, dispatch a battalion of angels to strike the enemy dead on the spot? Apparently not. Instead he said nothing, did nothing, allowed himself to be whipped, bullied and nailed up, and just died.

It was only years later, when I watched TV's *Kung Fu* series (in which the impossibly gentle, Buddhist-trained drifter David Carradine acts meek and humble in the Old West but can pull off the most blistering feats of martial-arts aggro when the need arises) that I realised how much I had wanted Christ to be a hero behind all the teacherish gentility. The heroism of transcendence, of turning the other cheek, even of divine redemption cuts little ice with the average tot.

And yet, even though he let us down, even though the

passivity and gracefulness of his final hours struck the childish soul as unbearably pathetic, there was something about that martyred gaze, on the way to Calvary, that had a power of its own. Years before we wanted to play Hamlet in the shadow of the inner-city housing estate, lots of us wanted to play Christ, raising blood-streaked eyes to those of Joseph of Arimathea and signifying, through some magnanimous, Olympian gesture, that he may carry our cross; or having your face wiped by St Veronica, on whose own face the sympathy of the world is etched, and it's all for you.

Every small boy whose response to criticism was to plan to run away, join the army, get shot fighting for Queen and country and die in the bosom of a grieving family (who would at last realise – just too late – his true worth), every small victim-figure has at some point thought of embracing that delicious martyrdom. Some of them have gone on doing so ever since.

The central image from the TV Passion – that of the enemy's torches flaming in procession through the night as they arrived to take our hero away – resonated through every part of my child's-eye view of the Church. It was Us against Them. Them – they – inhabited the darkness, wailing like banshees, threatening like wolves or nocturnal soldiery, fearsome and always lying in wait. We, on the other hand, were warm and safe indoors, snugly wrapped in the blanket of home, protected by faith and love from the ravages of the ghostly emissaries from Hell.

The core of a Catholic family, like the interior of a Catholic home, was an intense heat of passionate partisanship, as heavy smelling as a Jewish or Italian kitchen, as richly textured as the mutton stew with dumplings we ate for lunch every Saturday.

For Catholicism engaged all the senses. Its frightening intensity, its promise of damnation or bliss for ever, its requirement of eternal vigilance, seemed woven into the usual sense-data of childhood: the smell of sausages cooking in a scullery full of

WENDY PERRIAM

At my secondary school I was very devout. It was encouraged – the more devout you were, the more you were rewarded. I'd go to Mass and Benediction every day, sometimes go a third time. To show your devotion you were expected to give up everything, to wash in freezing water, to put pebbles in your shoes. I was a perfectionist, and I wanted to be better at giving up than anyone else. So at mealtimes, I remember, I'd try to take the smallest or just the worst piece in the serving dish because I was so devout. In fact I wanted to be a nun. You soon realised that the best students were being creamed off to become nuns – marriage was considered very much a second-rate thing to do.

shadows with a crucifix on the wall; the memory of firelight on the brass and mahogany coal-scuttle as the Rosary murmurously moved on to the next decade; the sound of the convent school choir soaring through the hymn 'Star of the Sea' with its Homeric imagery of tempests and banners of darkness.

The smell of sweet incense, charcoal and thick red wine that clung headily around you when – the youngest incense-carrying 'boat boy' ever to appear on the altar – you emerged from serving a seventy-minute High Mass. The taste of the Communion wafer that meant God was lying on your tongue, about to be ingested body and soul within you – it tasted less a wafer than some papery membrane, slightly flavoured, that melted on the roof of your mouth.

The touch of priestly hands completes the sensory picture. Priests had mystical hands, bestowing blessings that carried the authority of God himself. They were leathery hands or flabbily wet hands, eloquently expressive hands or crabbily gnarled old claws, but their priestliness gave them a sort of added value. If a priest touched you it was special, so you looked in everyday wonder at those bitten, grown-up fingers and wondered through what chasms of experience their owner had been in order to emerge so ennobled on the far side.

Everyday wonder, indeed. While non-Catholic children noted, then forgot, the details of the world around them, and while they might be reasonably content one day and averagely disgruntled the next, we grew up constantly amazed at the world: at the Devil and God, and his Beloved Son who had died most horribly to save us, because we were instinctively wicked (the fault of distant ancestors), and must try to expiate our sinfulness though it meant watching our every move with the vigilance of a prison guard, for fear that we would burn in the pits of Hell beyond imaginable time . . . it's quite a lot for a short-trousered neurotic to handle all at once. It gave us pictures in our heads – of death and salvation, Hell and Heaven, the massed ranks of angels and the divisions of demons – that no cynicism, no lapsing of faith nor all the clueless amorality of the real world could ever shift.

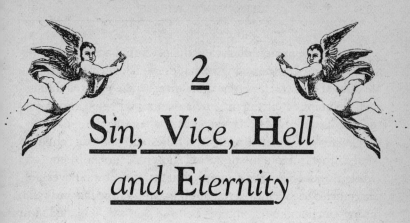

2
Sin, Vice, Hell
and Eternity

THIS IS HOW YOU GROW UP. When you are an infant the only abstractions you can handle are of people, pleasant or unpleasant. When you become a child, notions of place – again, pleasant or otherwise – become equally potent or more so. When you're a little older, the more fragile concept of time enters your thought-system as you learn to relate the minutes and years to scraps of your own life. And lastly (the theory concludes) you get to the biggest abstractions of all: ethics, morals, empathy, wisdom.

The Catholic child starts with the Devil. You're told that, unless you do what is right (or, interchangeably, do what you're told) a hideous man with vile powers and insinuating ways will come and get you. When you've matured so far that you are no longer frightened of nursery bogey-men, they hit you with Hell. If the ghastly imagery of roasting flesh and prodding spikes should start to pall in your mind, it means you're ready to be haunted by the idea of eternity. And when you start to understand the vastness of eternity, it somehow doesn't matter whether it's Heaven or Hell; they're both equally, mind-stretchingly frightening.

It is a phenomenon of the Catholic Church that the largest abstractions, of virtue and vice, good and evil, right and wrong, are dinned into you from the start, when you're too young to be sophisticated about them, and remain immovably lodged in your psyche all your life. The reason is simple: beneath the apparently simple duality of 'right and wrong' lies the terrifyingly vivid opposition of God and the Devil, closely followed by that of Heaven and Hell. Such grand reward for virtue and brutal punishment of vice means you never forget to wonder about your behaviour.

The Manichean opposition of flesh and spirit was, as far as the Catholics are concerned, a heresy. But the Church itself uses a similar primary-colour division between the world of God and righteousness and the pit of wrong-doing and Hell. The crucial catch was that you could easily fall into this terminal pit, not through being constitutionally evil or unrepentantly immoral, but simply through yielding to temptation, being swayed by bad company, by a moment's lack of vigilance in the middle of a war zone.

Growing up Catholic starts and ends in learning virtues and spurning vices. Like other religions it is (for the young adherent at any rate) almost exclusively concerned with behavioural ethics. But it supports with a backbone of steel any benign, goody-goody injunctions about living a life of 'Christian virtues'. Be good, it says in effect, *or else*. All the paraphernalia of sacramental ritual, of Mass and Confession, of prayers and pilgrimage and sermons and retreats, had at its base an insistence that living in a certain way will get you to the supreme reward of Heaven. It was always possible to hear that the converse was also being said: that living in this way was your only sure chance of avoiding Hell.

JUDGMENT DAY

These were weighty notions for a child to deal with. Perhaps the weightiest of all was the idea of the Last Judgment. Death meant little to us (I felt it must be like falling down in the playground, only for much longer than usual) except as a transitional stage to Heaven or Hell. But Judgment Day, that unimaginably vast exam, that mortifying interview before the celestial headmaster – it made your hair stand on end.

For one thing, it meant the end of the world. This was the idea: sometime, God would put a stop to things, as though declaring an innings, and the dead would rise again and be reunited with their souls. All the human beings who ever lived on earth would then mill about waiting to be consigned to Eternal Damnation, Eternal Bliss or the temporary Alcatraz of Purgatory. It was an awesome thought, as was the thought of the world ending. There would, we were told, be signs: great wars, great famines, the coming of an Antichrist, the darkening of the sun and moon, the appearance in the sky of a fiery cross . . . it was the Book of Revelations directed by Ken Russell. We silently added a few scenes – huge armadas with their sails in rags, crumbling mountain peaks, great Homeric harbours full of light and action, suddenly darkened.

Every Catholic remembers at least one day when the sky turned grey, then black at mid-morning, when it seemed likely to rain for ever, when thunderstorms crashed and rampaged overhead, and you thought (no, you were certain) that the end of the world had come. It had arrived unannounced, as promised, and a damn sight too early. It was awful to be taken by surprise. Like certain mothers who insist that you shouldn't leave home without clean underpants in case you're knocked down by a truck and taken to hospital, you were desperately afraid of being caught short, far from a confessional, and with not even a four-minute warning to alert you (although those fiery crosses in the sky should be a dead giveaway).

We were never sure about the rising of the dead. Surely, we thought, you go to Heaven or Hell when you die? Why the Day of Judgment, except for the people living at the time? Did it really mean that when you died your body lay in the ground until the Last Judgment? And if so, where did your soul go? This unconscionable period between death and Judgment – was it like being *remanded in custody*? And what, oh what, of the Judgment itself? It would be a ledger several miles high and slightly fewer wide, the pages of which would turn with the minatory crackle of massive, prehistoric leaves. It would take several of the judge's guards (God himself wouldn't be the judge; He would wait behind a screen, like Santa Claus, to greet the winners) would turn each page until your name appeared, followed by a list as long as the Thames of everything you did wrong in your lifetime. They would know it all, so there was no use trying to cover up. There would be a tick alongside each sin you actually confessed and were forgiven; and an angry red cross for each one that remained unshriven. The judge (sort of Pontius Pilate, without the charm) would keep pursing his lips, shaking his head, and giving sharp whistled little intakes of breath as he weighed your chances of getting round *this* one . . . A no-win situation if there ever was.

HEAVEN AND HELL

Gather a roomful of Catholics together and ask them for their childhood picture of Heaven and their view of it today, and you'll get nowhere. Ask the same question about Hell, and you will have your ear bent for the rest of the afternoon. Nobody knows why this is. Catholics are told about the delights of Heaven from their earliest age, but cannot visualise it and do not much care for it. It's as if they reserve all their goggle-eyed imaginings for the Other Place. And it reveals, incidentally, the relative potency of the stick and the carrot in Catholic lives.

Heaven, we were told, was both a physical place and a state of mind. It was the place and state of everlasting happiness in the next life. It was conceived as a true and natural home, which you would share with God. It was, naturally, up in the sky, well above the highest clouds, a floating island like Gulliver's Laputa. Its chief happiness, we learned, lay in beholding the face of God in all His grandeur and beauty, although not, presumably, all the time. It is a place to which we were once entitled (until Adam and Eve lost the right to it for themselves and everyone who came after) to which we are again made heirs by the sacrament of Baptism. Other interpretations might be added. Heaven is seen as a country, a single patch of green-sward like the Garden of Eden (which was seriously thought of as having an earthly location, somewhere around Damascus), a spiritual state, a gathering of congenial souls (as though at a non-violent football match) but also a place of perfect independent happiness and contentment.

These days I have a clearer view than when young of what it must be like: Heaven is an unbelievably huge cocktail party, with a guest list of everybody you ever knew or liked, plus a few interesting strangers thrown in as a bonus (perhaps they've drifted over from someone else's blissful throng). Every single resident of Heaven will simultaneously be having his or her own party (an appalling problem of logistics, but they can do this sort of thing in Heaven), exchanging gossip and clinking glasses in the middle of a vast open plain, overseen, as on a gigantic video screen, by the beaming face of God, as he nods politely to all the guests and occasionally murmurs that there's plenty of food in the kitchen . . .

There is, sadly, a flaw in this otherwise pleasing vision. There would be in Heaven no need for food or drink, since there's no such thing as hunger or thirst up there. There wouldn't be any gossip (nothing very interesting anyway) because nobody would be behaving badly, and nobody in Heaven would be malicious enough to talk about it even if they were. Nobody would be in need of help, nobody would be capable of getting upset or making a fool of themselves, nobody would be anything but perfectly contented. It threatens to be a terrible let-down after a lifetime of striving to be good. Heaven must just be a place of total equilibrium and perfect boredom.

Many Catholics believe that you will get your body back when you reach Heaven. The disintegrated flesh will knit back together and you'll stand there, a palpable physical presence, as good as new. But will you look old or young or middle-aged? Will you look like your last passport photo? Will you start off young and gradually age, only more gracefully than you did last time? (Surely not – you can't keep doing that for all eternity.) Will you be reconstituted looking as you did when you died? But imagine all the ill faces, the frail geriatric bones, the ghastly on-the-point-of-death looks of horror that would be perpetuated.

My mother maintained that you would be re-born 'looking in your prime' or otherwise at your best, looking grown-up but not yet old – looking, in other words, as people would like to remember you. But, I protested, that means everyone in Heaven would look about the same age. That'd be fine with me, she replied. But it would also mean, I persisted, that her father and grandfather (and I myself, come to that) would all stand around, aged about forty, with no sense of seniority nor family hierarchy. 'What are you talking about?' she said witheringly. 'Wouldn't I introduce you?'

There aren't any jokes in Hell, but there's a lot of other things. The most terrifying description of the 'place or state' is to be found in Joyce's *Portrait of the Artist as a Young Man*, when Stephen listens to a retreat sermon by the visiting Father Arnall. It's an overwhelming tirade of Gothic invention, that Joyce allegedly borrowed from a medieval Italian tract.

───────────────JAMES JOYCE───────────────

A holy saint (one of our own fathers I believe it was) was once vouchsafed a vision of Hell. It seemed to him that he stood in the midst of a great hall, dark and silent save for the ticking of a great clock. The ticking went on unceasingly; and it seemed to this saint that the sound of the ticking was the ceaseless repetition of the words – ever, never; ever, never. Ever to be in Hell, never to be in Heaven; ever to be shut off from the presence of God, never to enjoy the beatific vision; ever to be eaten with flames, gnawed by vermin, goaded with burning spikes, never to be free from those pains; ever to have the conscience upbraid one, the memory enrage, the mind filled with darkness and despair, never to escape; ever to curse and revile the foul demons who gloat fiendishly over the misery of their dupes, never to behold the shining raiment of the blessed spirits; ever to cry out of the abyss of fire to God for an instant, a single instant, of respite from such awful agony, never to receive, even for an instant, God's pardon; ever to suffer, never to enjoy; ever to be damned, never to be saved; ever, never; ever, never. O, what a dreadful punishment! An eternity of endless agony, of endless bodily and spiritual torment, without one ray of hope, without one moment of cessation, of agony limitless in intensity, of torment infinitely varied, of torture that sustains eternally that which it eternally devours, of anguish that everlastingly preys upon the spirit while it racks the flesh, an eternity, every instant of which is itself an eternity of woe. Such is the terrible punishment decreed for those who die in mortal sin by an almighty and a just God.

Hell is a cramped and airless prison, reeking of the worst, most unbreathable stench in the world, roasting with flames that eternally burn in pitch darkness, furiously raging for ever, while the damned scream and howl unceasing curses at each other for getting to this state. They are attended by mocking devils of unspeakable ugliness who will work as your conscience and say things like, 'I told you so. Why didn't you listen?' while prodding you with goads and spikes. If that weren't enough, there's the spiritual punishment: the damned will finally see exactly what and how much they've lost in losing God. The remorse of conscience will afflict them over and over again, as they fruitlessly try (too late) to repent . . . And so on. Re-read it when you've grown up and it still puts the fear of God into you. You have to go and lie down for a while and pray, once again, that it isn't true.

KAREN ARMSTRONG

I was terrified of Hell. It gave me an awful sense of endless loss. I had dreams of the Last Day, the holocaust that awaited. I kept performing mortal sins. I lost my bus fare but found a penny and didn't give it to the nuns. Well, it felt like big-time larceny. When I went to Confession I didn't confess that so every subsequent Communion I made was a blasphemy.

FRANK O'CONNOR

Then, to crown my misfortunes, I had to make my first Confession and Communion. It was an old woman called Ryan who prepared us for these; she was well-to-do, lived in a big house on Montenotte, wore a black cloak and bonnet, and came every day to school at three o'clock when we should have been going home, and talked to us of Hell. She may have mentioned the other place as well, but that could only have been by accident, for Hell had the first place in her heart.

She lit a candle, took out a new half-crown, and offered it to the first boy who would hold one finger – only one finger! – in the flame for five minutes by the school clock. Being always very ambitious I was tempted to volunteer, but I thought it might look greedy. Then she asked were we afraid of holding one finger – only one finger! – in a little candle flame for five minutes and not afraid of burning all over in roasting hot furnaces for all eternity. 'All eternity! Just think of that! A whole lifetime goes by and it's nothing, not even a drop in the ocean of your sufferings.' The woman was really interesting about Hell, but my attention was all fixed on the half-crown. At the end of the lesson she put it back in her purse. It was a great disappointment; a religious woman like that, you wouldn't think she'd bother about a thing like a half-crown.

(from 'First Confession', published in My Oedipus Complex and Other Stories, Penguin, 1987)

PURGATORY

Purgatory was about as much as you could reasonably hope for. It was the ante-room to Heaven and the recovery room for those

who had narrowly missed Hell. It was where the bulk of the
'faithful departed' (i.e. believers in the Catholic faith who die in
a state of grace but have some unpunished venial sins still on
their soul) spend unknown portions of time before being finally
allowed to the Divine Presence.

You pictured the Purgatorial Ones as inhabiting a slightly
nicer dungeon than Hell – less smelly, less dark, less sadistic
warders, the flames at gas mark 5 rather than a roasting mark 9 –
and even thought of them as capable of happiness.

For one thing, they were assured that one day they would see
God, so could presumably count off the days until that final
liberation. For another, they had successive generations of
Catholics rooting for them on earth. Saying prayers for the holy
souls in Purgatory was a daily chore which made you feel better:
because, in your bountiful goodness, you were helping a complete stranger get sprung from jail and delivered to Heaven
(where presumably he or she would owe you a favour or two when
the time came . . .).

The souls in Purgatory were your friends and allies, stuck in a
kind of POW camp and needing your help to get out. Who had
put them there? Why, the judgment of our merciful God had
decreed them insufficiently good or apologetic about their shortcomings to join him just yet. Immediately one sensed a split of
loyalties. Does God hate the holy souls while they are in
Purgatory, only to love them once they reach Heaven? Whose
side is He on? No, no, came the reply, He loves the souls in
Purgatory, but as well as being loving and merciful He is a just
God and His justice demands they be completely 'purified' before
being admitted into His presence. We were unimpressed. He
sounded like someone who'd demand you wiped your feet before
besmirching his living-room.

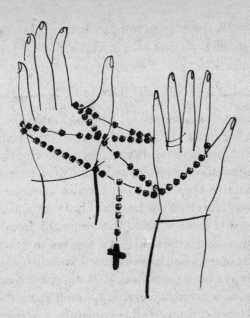

LIMBO

There was one other place you could go for all eternity: Limbo. This ludicrously named nightmare of tiny babies and prehistoric pagans was hardly a more attractive proposition than Purgatory. I hated the whole idea of it, and many Catholics still remember regarding it with revulsion.

Limbo was an extraordinary paradox – a nice part of Hell. It was the place where the souls of little babies who died unbaptised went for all eternity. If their parents fail to get them to a font or to administer Baptism themselves (the argument runs), the unredeemed infants are still in a state of original sin and cannot enter Heaven. It always seemed a strict and unfeeling way to treat a blameless infant. Was it a nice place or a nasty one? Disingenuously, it was described as a place where the babies would eternally enjoy a 'natural happiness' – like being under morphine sedation for ever and ever.

————————— JENNIFER JOHNSTON —————————

I have a very clear memory of the local curate, Mr Hanson, coming to the house one winter's evening and saying to my mother, 'I've just come to talk about Jennifer being confirmed.' My mother burst out laughing and said, 'She hasn't even been christened!' I was appalled at this because it carried a terrible social stigma, apart from the fact that I had within me the awful mythology of Limbo which I had acquired from Catholic friends. I was quite convinced that if between that moment and the moment of my being baptised I were to fall off my bike and be run over by a No 8 tram, I would go straight to Limbo where I would spend a horrible eternity. I wasn't going to take any chances: I stopped going to school on my bicycle for six weeks until the christening actually happened . . .

(from *A Portrait of the Artist as a Young Girl*, edited by John Quinn, Methuen, 1985)

The first use of the place was to house the souls of 'The Just' (viz., the might-have-been-faithfuls) of the pre-Christian era, who lived good lives but because of the timing of their birth had missed the opportunity to worship Christ (how smugly the Church claimed all the good people as their own). They stayed in Limbo when they died, waiting for the Resurrection and Redemption. Christ himself went there when he died; his soul stayed for forty days until his Ascension into Heaven. Whatever did he make of the spectacle of all those ignorantly blissful babies everywhere?

SIN

Up above the clouds Heaven lazily flew onwards, picking up a few privileged new inmates from time to time. Down below even the primeval murk lay the unspeakable wastes of Hell, into which far greater numbers were pitched every moment of every day. As soon as you were awake enough to know anything, you were made aware of this awesome split of locations.

What got you into Heaven was a blameless life, an essentially negative response to the thousands of opportunities for wrong-doing offered by the disgraceful state of the post-lapsarian world. What got you into Hell was an accumulation of crimes against God. They were collectively called sin.

DAVID LODGE

Up there was Heaven; down there was Hell. The name of the game was Salvation, the object to get to Heaven and avoid Hell. It was like Snakes and Ladders. Sin sent you plummeting down towards the pit; the sacraments, good deeds, acts of self-mortification, enabled you to climb back towards the light. Everything you did or thought was subject to spiritual account-ing. It was either good, bad or indifferent. Those who suc-ceeded in the game eliminated the bad and converted as much of the indifferent as possible into the good. For instance, a banal bus journey (indifferent) could be turned to good account by silently reciting the Rosary, unobtrusively fingering the beads in your pocket as you trundled along. To say the Rosary openly and aloud in such a situation was more problematical. If it witnessed to the faith, even if it excited the derision of non-believers (providing they were borne with patience and fore-giveness) it was, of course, good — indeed heroically virtuous;

but if done to impress others, to call attention to your virtue, it was worse than indifferent, it was bad – spiritual pride, a very slippery snake. Progress towards Heaven was full of such pitfalls. On the whole, a safe rule of thumb was that anything you positively disliked doing was probably good, and anything you liked doing enormously was probably bad, or potentially bad – an 'occasion of sin'.

(from *How Far Can You Go?*, Secker, 1980)

You were assured that you had started your life already full of inherited sin, from whose worst effects you had been narrowly redeemed by Baptism. The only reason you weren't already heading Hell-wards was the prescience of your parents and the potency of the First Sacrament. From now on, though, for all of the life that lay before you, it was up to you to watch what you were doing every day. As with English law, it was no use pleading ignorance. That would be no defence at the Last Judgment. The temptations of Satan lay all around you; you had to monitor your every move to make sure you weren't transgressing God's law.

The New Testament had provided a handy but over-generalised guide to wrong behaviour, called the Ten Commandments. Three of them ('I am the Lord thy God, thou shalt not have false gods before me'; 'Thou shalt not take the name of the Lord Thy God in vain'; 'Remember that thou keep holy the Sabbath Day') were concerned with the Lord. The remaining seven were about human behaviour in society, the operations of men and women towards each other. Looked at dispassionately, they seem no more than rules for the orderly conduct of any social organism: if everybody told lies or killed each other willy-nilly, or stole from each other as a matter of course, things would break down completely, whether in Birmingham or Uttar Pradesh.

What the Catholic Church did was interpret the Commandments for you, to bring a strict, decisive rigour to the airy generalities. 'Thou shalt not commit adultery' and 'Thou shalt not covet thy neighbour's wife' were the most widely interpreted: these two simple injunctions were made to accommodate a whole raft of secondary considerations, from self-abuse to reading *Fanny Hill*. 'Thou shalt not bear false witness against thy neighbour', a straightforward ban on calumnious tittle-tattle, was reinterpreted to include lies of any sort. 'Thou shalt not kill' came to include grievous bodily harm, quarrelling, anger, feelings of revenge, scandal and 'bad example', one of those strangely marginal sins which the perpetrator is extremely likely to be unaware of committing.

At no time did you receive an actual list of what the Church deemed sinful: instead you had to 'examine your conscience' and then you'd know. Terrific. This meant that following your instincts and doing things that seemed right or pleasurable had constantly to be held up to the judgment of an unknown, or at best dimly glimpsed, internal jury. The total effect was to floor you with guilt. Sometimes it seemed that everything was wrong or bad or suspect: not working hard enough at school, thinking your Aunt Maud was a hideous old bag, wishing you had a toy grenade launcher like your friend Harry, saying 'Damn' . . . Anything you did which was not surrounded by a rosy glow of righteousness suddenly pitched you into a mire of uncertainties.

Sin took as many forms as there are modes of action. You could sin consciously or unconsciously, sin by inaction as much as by action, sin just by being in a situation that might lead to sinfulness. The Catechism informed you that certain classes of sin existed, the super-terrible ones like Murder and the spiritual ones such as Despair and Presumption. And for those whose heads were by now spinning with guilt, the Church kindly divided the sins you were likely to commit into two strengths or intensities: you could commit a 'mortal' sin, or just a 'venial' one.

Venial Sins

Venial sins were the minnows of transgression, the small, humdrum, everyday acts in which you turned away from God or his earthly representatives. They were mostly instances of dis-obedience (to parents or teachers), of disrespect (ditto but also in disrespect to God by abusing his name or saying 'bloody' which is a contraction – we were told – of 'By Our Lady') and of what was really no more than pernicious wool-gathering but came under the heading of 'entertaining impure thoughts'.

Venial sins were indistinguishable from 'being naughty'. They weren't the sort of things people went to prison for. Nobody was meant to take them seriously after a certain age. They existed to keep delinquents like us in check by encouraging self-analysis and self-prosecution.

Mortal Sins

Mortal sins, on the other hand, were The Business, the real thing. They had ghastly consequences: if you committed a mortal sin and died, you'd go straight to Hell and no questions asked – no remission, no plea-bargaining, no court of appeal. You'd absolutely had it.

All sin, we learned, put a stain on the soul, which had been – and could be again – whiter than white. A venial sin was a scuff on the spiritual boot, an ink blot on the divine manuscript of the Catholic self, a blackhead on one's clear, holy complexion. You got rid of it by going to Confession, expressing true (and often genuine) remorse, vowing not to do it again and working your porridge of a few prayers. Nothing to it.

Mortal sins were infinitely worse disruptions of the soul's vulnerable organ. They were atrocious excrescences like rotting black cabbages, huge cancerous growths on the spiritual body, ulcerous and deadly. They could – provided you headed like greased lightning for a confessional as soon as possible after committing one – be forgiven too, but that didn't mean you could get complacent. In this moral launderette, the soul comes out white and gleaming time after time, because the Lord is merciful even to the least worthy of his charges. But you had to work at being sorry.

The priest would make sure you were given an especially hard time over a mortal sin, under the guise of explaining the seriousness of your felony. This was to make you feel very small and very bad. Your penance would be large (but not as large as you'd gladly be given – several Rosaries, Mass every day for a month, a pilgrimage to Knock), your repentance fevered and weepingly sincere, your determination never to do it again (and to give yourself up to the law if necessary) unstinting. Because otherwise you don't get off, you don't get absolved and you could still go to Hell for eternity that very night . . .

Mortal sins were death to the soul, and the most obvious mortal sin was murder. Prostitution was a racing certainty for a mortal sin. Armed robbery was pretty clearly mortal. Invading a neutral country was presumed to be mortal. Stealing huge sums from charities devoted to children or cripples could hardly be anything but mortal. The same went for the torture of small babies. But after that, a fog tended to come down over our imaginations. We simply ran out of ideas for things that were likely to count as soul-destroying. How innocent we were.

Reserved Sins

Occasionally one would hear, from worldlier members of the class or from ancient Irish relations, of something called 'reserved sins' that were especially bad. We longed to know more. Worse than mortal, huh? What possible outermost extremes of grossness could these be?

Rumour had it that to read certain books (mostly by the Marquis de Sade) you had to visit the British Library under a kind of armed guard, apply in quintuplicate, wait for weeks in a draughty ante-room preparing oneself through meditation for the moral ordeal ahead, then be grudgingly allowed a half-hour's peek at the abominations detailed therein, the whole time under the supervision of the library's trustees, themselves overseen by a stern-faced bishop in full canonicals. Apparently (we told each other in hushed confidence) the goings-on between hard covers were reserved sins because they couldn't be forgiven or absolved by ordinary priests; they were reserved for the higher echelons of the Church and states to deal with.

Once, with great excitement, I heard my father mention an Irish couple who had both been accused of such a sin, and had to take their case to the Bishop of Galway. Both together? Simultaneously? Gosh, you mean they were doing something, you know, in bed, something so dreadful . . . ? The truth was a terrible let-down. They were guilty of sending their son to the distinguished, but Protestant, Trinity College Dublin. The rural pastors weren't having any of their flock putting the next generation of Catholics in the way of the opposition . . .

SIN – THE CATHOLIC LEAGUE TABLE

Original Sin

Nothing you can do about it. You didn't choose to commit it – your ancestor Adam did. Everyone is born with it on his/her conscience, to be shriven by Baptism, the First Sacrament and First Absolution. And what precisely was the original sin? Disobedience to the Lord, when Adam ate an apple from the Forbidden Tree at the behest of the Devil. This is the first time you'll hear the word 'disobedience' kicked around in Catholic rubric – but very far from the last.

Capital Sins

These represent the ground rules of vice and virtue, as the Catholic Church sees them. They're the empirical, temperamental qualities which lead (we were told) to sin and wrongdoing; and they're always mentioned along with their counterbalancing virtues. They're also known as the Seven Deadly Sins:

Pride	*whose equivalent virtue is*	**Humility**
Covetousness	*whose equivalent virtue is*	**Liberality**
Lust	*whose equivalent virtue is*	**Chastity**
Anger	*whose equivalent virtue is*	**Meekness**
Gluttony	*whose equivalent virtue is*	**Temperance**
Envy	*whose equivalent virtue is*	**Brotherly Love**
Sloth	*whose equivalent virtue is*	**Diligence**

Sub-Venial Sins

A.k.a. little-old-lady sins. Confessed by the super-virtuous as make-weights to an otherwise threadbare narrative.

✛ Missing a decade from one's evening Rosary.
✛ Experiencing feelings of irritation about a) supermarket managers, b) chat-show hosts, c) social workers.
✛ Failing to attend Mass on the Feast of St Nicholas of Flue.
  Failing to relinquish one's bus seat to someone even more decrepit.
✛ Entertaining thoughts of Sir Alistair Burnet during the Sunday sermon.
✛ Saying 'Blast' and 'Bother'.
✛ Guilt at being unable to contribute several thousand pounds to African charities, due to paltriness of state pension and disability allowance.
✛ Being in great pain, and failing to offer it up for the Holy Souls.

Sins Against the Holy Spirit

These vague little items are miles removed from the standard, concrete forms of sin. They're about spiritual wrong-doing, and are a little marginal for our purposes.

✛ Presumption (thinking you're one of the chosen and will therefore get into Heaven by a kind of divine right).
✛ Despair (giving up all hope of getting into Heaven and thus failing to trust in God's magnanimity).
✛ Resisting the Known Truth.
✛ Envy of another's spiritual good.
✛ Obstinacy in sin.
✛ Final Impenitence.

Venial Sins

These leave a stain on the soul, removable only through sanctifying grace. Fair-to-middling everyday transgressions. To err is human etc. . . .

✛ Saying 'Fuck!' and 'Bugger!' and 'Jesus Wept!'.
✛ Minor fraud (dodgy expenses claims, wilful concealments from the Inland Revenue).
✛ Minor theft (stealing not more than five per cent of the victim's weekly wage; pinching office stapler, borrowing money, clothes, library books and not returning).
✛ Entertaining impure thoughts of Greta Scacchi, Edwina Currie, Cardinal Hume, Mickey Rourke etc. Details of exactly *who* it was aren't, for some reason, generally required.
✛ Getting drunk.
✛ Being disobedient to parents, teachers, priests, scoutmaster/ Brown Owl.
✛ Showing disrespect (audible or physical) towards elders and betters.
✛ Trying to unfasten clothing of opposite sex.
✛ Arriving at Mass after the Gospel/leaving Mass before Communion.
✛ Allowing oneself to feel jealous, envious, covetous and consequently murderous towards fellow man with Porsche and compact disc player.
✛ Neglecting to visit the sick/clothe the naked/feed the hungry.
✛ Reading impure books (by Lawrence, Miller, Donleavy, Robbins, J. Collins)
✛ and attending immodest movies and plays (*Women in Love*, $9\frac{1}{2}$ *Weeks*, *Ai No Corrida*, *Oh Calcutta*, *Once a Catholic* especially fine examples).

✞ Failing to fast and abstain on the relevant days of the Church calendar.

✞ Taking drugs.

Mortal Sins

The big ones. Mortal sins kill the soul and, should you die after committing one, will send you straight to Hell for ever and ever.

✞ Fornication, i.e. extra-marital sex. No excuses (ignorance, wartime romance, belief in imminence of marriage, feelings of pity etc.).

✞ Breaking of solemn vows, oaths and similar deals with God.

✞ Causing actual or grievous bodily harm.

✞ Major theft (appropriating more than five per cent of person's wages, holding up bank, stealing car, burglary, dishonestly handling etc.).

✞ Wilful blasphemy/encouraging others in disrespect for the Church.

✞ Worship of false gods (while being a Catholic at the same time).

✞ Prostitution.

✞ Bestiality.

✞ Masturbation.

✞ Starting an Unjust War.

✞ Mugging.

✞ Perjury in court while under oath.

✞ Attempting to deprave and/or corrupt the young by publishing or

✞ broadcasting material deemed immodest by the Board of Censors.

✞ Dealing in hard drugs.

✞ Failing to attend Mass on Sundays and Holydays of Obligation.

Super-Mortal Sins

The really over-the-top ones. Also known as the 'sins crying to Heaven for vengeance'. There are just four:

✣ Wilful murder.
✣ Sodomy.
✣ Oppression of the poor.
✣ Defrauding labourers of their wages.

Note the hint of trades-union fundamentalism about the third and fourth of these special-category sins. They're directed most pointedly at autocratic bosses, bullying foremen, corrupt tax officials and greedy fat cats.

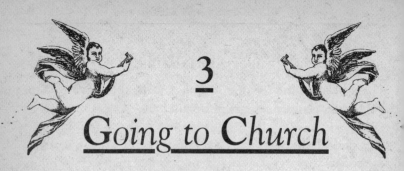

3

Going to Church

THE FIRST TIME YOU NOTICE that you're a Catholic is when you find yourself going quietly crazy at Mass. You are very young. You would like to play with something or somebody. You would like to be in the garden stomping on a few ants or poking a new stick into an interesting drain. Instead you are in a big vaulted cavern of a church, with lots of tweed jackets and gaberdine coats standing up and sitting down in random, unsettling order.

It is uncomfortably hot. A smokily sweet smell that you will come to know as incense drifts through the congregation and makes you feel sick. You cannot talk or read or draw pictures or pick your nose or go to sleep. Instead you are instructed to direct your attention at three men on a stage performing some recondite act. One is very tall and glittery, dressed in a rhinestone-encrusted ballgown emblazoned with a rudimentary fish. On either side of him, two midgets in white lace frocks glide about and ring bells.

'What are they doing now, Mummy?' you enquire.

'Shhhh, darling, it's the Consecration.'

'What's he doing with his hands?'

'He's elevating the Host. Say "My Lord and my God".'

'My Lord and My God.'

'Good boy.'

And once again, incomprehension gave way to a strategic obedience.

Joining the army of the Lord meant that your basic training started early. At a time when non-Catholic tinies were goggling at Beatrix Potter or taking a first tumble from their shiny red tricycles, we were plunged into a dense, time-absorbing network of Church ritual.

Wherever you looked, some religious event was always being celebrated or anticipated. It was far more than a matter of putting in an appearance at Christmas and Easter. Each of these two colossal events was preceded by weeks of preparation, of sub-sectional devotions with their own incidental rituals: All Souls' Night, Advent, Passion Sunday, Palm Sunday, Shrove Tuesday, the wonderfully named Spy Wednesday . . . And through the

remainder of the year, religion loomed in the background of everything you did. We seemed to be always on the way to Church, in Church, or hanging around outside Church.

For children everywhere, in all denominations, Church is a magnificent bore, a crashingly dull alternative to play. But the Catholic child is special because he or she knows there is no other possible course of action. You have to go to Mass on a Sunday in the same way that you have to breathe in and out to remain alive. It's not even a matter for discussion. You know that, somewhere, it says not going to Sunday Mass is a mortal sin – but you shouldn't need to be told. It's one of the strongest foundation-stones of your faith. What would happen to you if you just stayed at home one Sunday? Strangely, it was a question no one asked. The possible repercussions were too dreadful to contemplate.

Likewise, you didn't *have* to go to everything, but somehow you naturally did. As well as Sundays, you were bound to attend Mass on Holydays of Obligation. Your presence was expected at Confession every two or three weeks. 'It's as well not to leave it too long between visits', they would tell you, cannily implying that the longer you stayed away from the confessional, the greater your chances of being knocked down by a truck while awash with sin, and going straight to Hell. Not mandatory, but hardened by practice into becoming inevitable, was the Saturday morning trip to Mass at St Mary's a couple of miles away, and Saturday evenings at the Novena service. On Sundays, in addition, you were expected to sit through a glum Benediction at six p.m.

If you had any half-way serious desires to enter the more charmed circles of Catholic devoutness, you ringed in your diary the first Friday of each month, and attended Mass on that day: doing the Nine Fridays, as it was called, brought untold blessings upon you.

It came to operate like a drug, the habit of Mass. It made you feel grown-up for the first time. It gave you a strange new private life of communing with the Ineffable that made you feel both very devout and very important. I miss it still. One particularly strong memory was of rising at 6.30 a.m. on freezing mornings in March and April to attend Mass every day of Lent before going to school. It wasn't quite as simple as it sounds. No one else in the house was stirring. You had to creep around for fear of waking anyone. Breakfast was out of the question. Downstairs, opening the kitchen door on to drifts of sleet or barrages of hailstones, you left the radio cheerily playing something from the Top Ten (on the occasion I recall it was 'The Legend of Xanadu' by Dave Dee, Dozy, Beaky, Mick and Tich) and headed out into the grim streets, to a church where you'd be lucky to see a single other member of the congregation at the seven a.m. Mass.

I wish I could say it was simple self-righteousness. But it wasn't. There was something ennobling and glorious about the downbeat ceremonials, the yawning priest, the chill in your feet. You found you could pray with ease and fluency as though continuing the conversation (with God) of a lengthy friendship. You were suddenly on top of things, looking down on your life from some transcendent height and bursting with confidence. To be devout, to believe in the Creation, and to nod approval at the idea of obedience and self-discipline, all seemed the only right and proper approach to your future life. What a very *sober* thirteen-year-old I must have seemed.

There was a natural transition between being an earnestly devout member of the congregation and heading for the priest-hood (a process which represented a gradual approach to the sacred mysteries on the altar, like playing Grandmother's Foot-steps with the tabernacle). Between the two, however, there was another stage: I became an altar server. At school, I served Mass in the chapel, waiting on the Jesuit headmaster like (or so I

imagined) an imperturbable butler. At home in Battersea, I rose
through the ranks of servers at St Vincent's Church to become
'MC', a kind of Permanent Secretary to the celebrant of High
Mass. It's a very classy act (perhaps a better analogy would be to
find yourself playing the all-knowing Grand Vizier to a dozy
pasha) and one that confirms the strange theatrical quality that
hangs around the Catholic Church.

My friend Paul taught me the moves and scoffed at my
incompetence. Gradually we formed a partnership, and glided
around the altar perfectly in tandem, like Dowell and Sibley,
Astaire and Rogers . . . We became like Harley Street con-
sultants. We were in demand. Such was our standing at the
school, we were invited to the Jesuit HQ at Farm Street to serve
at some arcane Christmas ritual for which special new moves had
to be learned quickly (it sounded sinister and Masonic, but
wasn't really). We were asked to officiate (that's how we saw it)
at the Reparatrice Convent in Wimbledon for their Easter Vigil
Mass. Our assistance was requested (along with the school choir)
when an Old Boy got married. Paul and John, Altar Servers to
the Gentry. We did weddings, funerals – practically everything
but bar mitzvahs . . .

By the age of ten, in consequence, I was a connoisseur of
Catholic churches. No clerical Pevsner could have savoured
such a variety of houses of God as I. Chapels, cathedrals, high-
church churches ('bells and smells'), low-church churches,
foreign *églises*, fusty Italian shrines, modern Irish ranch-style
ones with their uniquely horrible, trendy-vicar script on the
walls. I had, in addition, attended open-air Masses in Lourdes,
Mass on the stairs at home when the house was being blessed, an
impromptu Mass in a hotel room for a tightly squeezed gaggle of
pilgrims.

We came to regard the places as strange amalgams of the cosy
and the unsettling. There was a certain *smell* of Catholicism, a

rich and heavy pall of candlewax, sweet incense, cut flowers, damp tweed and high seriousness. It gathered round you like a cloak when you entered; and as you headed for your seat, a feeling compounded of sudden earnestness and old-fashioned smugness overcame you: you'd begin to walk as though taking part in a procession, as if you were somebody unusually grand . . .

_____ JENNIFER JOHNSTON _____

I was attracted to churches more by atmosphere than by any religious practice. I loved the smell and feel of a Catholic church. I infinitely preferred that to the antiseptic atmosphere and the emptiness of the Church of Ireland. When you walked up the aisle of that church our feet clattered on metal grilles and you felt terribly alone and confronted with God, whereas the Catholic Church was warm and embracing and I loved that. For many years a great friend and I used to go into Donnybrook Catholic Church on our way back from school. If we had any spare pennies we would light candles and sit there and look at people and think This is so lovely! We were sucked into the atmosphere.

Other nostalgically inclined Catholics recall, as the quintessence of their church memories, the sound of a Catholic congregation singing the 'Ave Maria', a strangely dirge-like extolling of the Mother of God, full of mournful progressions yoked together by a chorus that dwindles through a series of downward cadences:

> Immaculate Mary, our hearts are on fire
> That title so wondrous fills all our desire.
> Ave, ave, ave Maria,
> Ave, ave, ave Maria.

Despite its boredom quotient, this hymn never wanted for fans, never went out of fashion. It's the official Catholic pilgrimage hymn at Lourdes.

At Benediction, the twin hymns 'O Salutaris Hostia' and 'Tantum Ergo' were always sung, day in, day out, until one grew tired of them and they disappeared into the background; hearing them again today you're struck by how remarkably tuneless they seem, compared to the Protestants' Ancient and Modern collection. Also the tempo was so contrived that it was quite

impossible to sing either hymn at any rate faster than a funereal keening: you always felt you were trying to speed things up but being restrained by the organist. Catholic singing only ever showed itself to good effect at Christmas Midnight Mass.

The main image one drew from the relentless church-going, however, was of the altar. It loomed before you, a fabulous sanctum of ageless mysteries, a closed-off area of holiness both frightening and obscurely comforting, like a great whisper from a childhood dream. Because there was no single focus of attention for your eyes – the tabernacle was always closed – you never knew what you were looking at. Something was there all right, but it wasn't to be discerned by the usual sensory apparatus.

Whether at Westminster Cathedral, Brompton Oratory, the Sacred Heart in Wimbledon or St Mary's in Clapham, the altar, with its Gothic arches, its spiky towers and bulbous excrescences, its air of uplifting severity, drew your eyes back from any scrutiny of the aisles, the people in the Lady Chapel, the stone gargoyles in the ceiling, and hung in your imagination thereafter like the battlements of an unreachable fortress.

INDULGENCES: THE CATHOLIC REWARD SYSTEM

Why did we do it? How did we become so obsessive about going to church? What did we expect to get out of it?

Beyond the desire to be a good and virtuous Catholic lay a surprisingly mercenary incentive. We went out of enlightened self-interest. In much the same spirit with which one collected the tokens from Corn Flake packets, eventually to trade them in by post for a plastic tractor, one went about collecting merit points, to cash in against the Day of Judgment. The merit points were called 'indulgences'.

The word held no connotations of 'self-indulgence' in the

hedonistic sense. It meant that your time in Purgatory might be lessened under certain circumstances. You learned about indulgences in your Missal or prayer book. Underneath certain prayers, in parentheses, was an indication of what a single recitation would 'win' you: '200 days' indulgence'; '500 days' indulgence'; 'five years' indulgence'. Elsewhere you learned that going to a certain Mass on a certain day, or attending a service several times over a period of months, would get you even more 'days'. The idea was that, because of the sins you had already racked up in the ledger of Judgment Day – whether forgiven or not – you were due to spend some time in Purgatory (as is almost everybody). An indulgence granted you, in effect, time off for good behaviour.

It comfortingly promised that your sentence in the fires of Purgatory would be commuted by a specific number of days. Its official definition was 'The remission of temporal punishment due to sins already forgiven granted by the Church from her spiritual treasury', which left one wondering two things. First, the puzzling paradox of a sin that's already been forgiven but for which one still has to atone (it seemed, to say the least, a bit unfair). And second, the idea of a 'spiritual treasury', like some quasi-governmental slush fund from which shadowy ecclesiastical bureaucrats in High Places would issue bursaries and dodgy grants to save the undeserving souls of their friends.

The top prize was a 'plenary indulgence'. It was a full remission. It meant that you were allowed off all the days you would have spent in Purgatory atoning for the sins you'd committed and been forgiven for. Did it, then, mean a free passage straight into Heaven? We were never quite sure. The priests would muddy the waters a bit, hint that there were always the rags of a few unconfessed sins lying about in the otherwise pristine launderette of the soul, and no one could really hope to escape doing some time in the divine nick.

Plenary indulgences weren't lightly given. You had to work for them, usually over a period of time, attending the right services, going to Confession and Communion, doing everything just right. There was, though, one short-cut. By some loophole in the rubric, you were promised a plenary if you went to church several times on the same day (it was, as I recall, All Souls' Day) and said certain prayers each time. There was nothing to specify that you had to go home between times so, with rat-like cunning, we would pray at the end of the church, nip outside for five minutes, come back in, say the same prayers again, nip out again . . . until the requisite number of visits and prayers had got you paroled from Purgatory.

There was a catch, however. A plenary indulgence would only be of real use at the moment of your demise, wiping the slate clean there and then. A few minutes after you'd won this glorious reprieve (the chances were) you'd be up to your neck in sins once more . . .

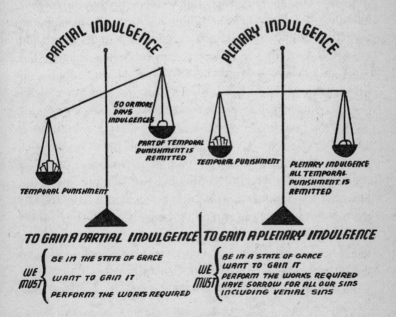

EXPOSITION OF THE
BLESSED SACRAMENT

Every so often, once or twice a year, the local church would announce 'the Forty Hours' Exposition', to take place over three days. There was no explanation of the reason for these periods of special devotion, but they were popular with the congregation in their low-key way. For one thing, there were indulgences a-plenty to be had just by dropping into the Church any time during the forty hours and saying a few prayers. For another, the Exposition was a striking sight to behold.

The Blessed Sacrament took the form of a Communion Host, extra-large size, encased in splendour inside a spiky gold and glass object called a 'monstrance'. This was carried in procession up and down the church aisle at the beginning and the end of the Exposition period. The idea, I suppose, was to give the population a proper sight of a genuinely holy and 'consecrated' object in which the essence of God was embodied. I remember being convinced I could see *something else beside the Host* in the monstrance as it drifted by my pew in a haze of incense, carried in the respectfully draped hands of the priest: could it have been a tiny attendant angel? There was no time to speculate or take a second look – and anyway you were supposed to bow your head in wonder at its approach, not kneel there gawping at it.

For the rest of the Exposition, the monstrance and its sacred freight sat on the altar, the only object on the pristine white cloth, and the congregation filed in, prayed directly to it, and left feeling much better. You prayed for the Holy Souls, the Faithful Departed, all your relations and the school dog. You begged the High King of Heaven to give you a break about some detail of your private life. You'd signed off with a whispered 'Cheerio' to the monstrance and whatever lay behind it. Nothing had happened to turn this one-directional diatribe into anything resembling a dialogue. It didn't matter. There was a communication of a kind in the tiny, unwavering white eye of the Sacrament a hundred yards away, as it seemed to look straight back at you. What did not reply was the answer to prayer.

PETITIONS AND PEP TALKS

By some unspoken tradition found among Catholic families, we would spend unconscionable hours of boredom hanging out beside the altar rails on Saturday mornings. First Mass, then Confession, then you lit a candle for the Souls in Purgatory. Next you trooped up to the side-altar where an image of Our Lady Of Perpetual Succour reposed in a blaze of candle-light. Before her, at ground level, among the ranks of kneeling forms, sat a wooden casket with a letter-box slot cut into the top; it resembled an antique ballot-box. Supplicants at this altar found a pad of paper, licked the pencil attached by a string and wrote, in the tiny space available, a petition to Our Lady. The slip was torn off, folded in four and posted in the box, eventually to be delivered, we assumed, through some supernatural mail-flap.

This curiously affecting little ritual – supposedly to reify one's desire for spiritual grace – was easy to ridicule, and the more desperate naughty boys occasionally asked that their temporarily ill-favoured little friends might catch bubonic plague and die. Others took it tremendously seriously, despite their lack of any mature spiritual dimension: petitions asking that the rugby first team would utterly crush King's School Wimbledon – our Protestant rivals at the top of the hill – were made in desperate good faith, and in the same quivering, last-hope tone of voice with which one would beg the Queen of Heaven for relief from the blazing thrall of acne.

On Saturday evenings, we'd all be back again at the same
church for the Novena, a matey but low-key devotional meeting
without any offerings of the sacraments. As the name implied, to
attend nine times in a row supposedly brought you special, if
unspecified, credits with the Most High (vid. sup.).

Apart from the singing, which for a Papist congregation was
generally enthusiastic and harmonious, the only human charm
of the proceedings lay in the sermon. Since the Novena was not
to be confused with Mass, the priest could not expatiate on the
significance of an event in the Catholic calendar, nor assist the
congregation in a close reading of the day's Lessons. Instead,
therefore, we had the Papist equivalent of the vicar's pastoral
visit or the padre's pep-talk to the men.

We were given case histories, little stories, telling anecdotes
about past parishioners: a saintly woman who, because her old
mother had fallen out of bed when she herself was away visiting a
sick friend, slowly declined into self-disgust; a young Clapham
tearaway redeemed by his love for a spirited 'modern girl' whose
church-going was an instinctive, natural part of her otherwise
'modern' lifestyle. The tone was mutedly inspirational. It
implied that, however bad or thoughtless or wicked, however
self-condemned and sinful we thought ourselves to be, there was
a higher and better state available to the meanest of us, only
just out of our grasp and to be reached through prayer or the
enlightenments of experience.

These were obscurely comforting messages to those among us
already consumed by guilt about our every action. It meant, for
one thing, that we still had a certain way to fall towards terminal
perdition and disgrace, before being rescued by some unbidden
succour from the angels.

MASS ETIQUETTE

It's only when you're accompanied to Mass by a non-Catholic friend that you realise precisely how much ritual and etiquette is involved. There's a routine to Church behaviour that's more stringent than diplomatic protocol. Many lapsed Catholics still instinctively make the Sign of the Cross when passing a church or overtaking a funeral; and if they were to enter a church now, for whatever reason, they would find it hard to advance many paces in any direction before the urge to genuflect overcame them. The rituals of physical behaviour become wholly instinctive and automatic. The following, for instance:

Holy water: just inside the church door, usually set into the wall there will be found a marble basin filled with none-too-clean water. Often the marble sides will be found to have worn away because of the thousands of fingers that have yearningly stabbed their way across the lip. You're supposed to dip your finger in the water and bless yourself (the cruciform blessing – forehead, sternum, left shoulder, right shoulder) every time you enter or leave a church. Sometimes a departing congregation will become logjammed around the exit as they all wait their turn at the marble font. They all have homes to go to; they will derive no obvious benefit from having three droplets of water trickle down their forehead; but they would no more think of missing this ritual gesture than of missing their lunch.

Genuflecting: that is, bending the knee as a mark of respect before the tabernacle containing the Blessed Sacrament (theoretically, that's also the reason why you bless yourself when passing a church – as though the Sacrament, from within its elaborate little house, were sending out a laser-like beam that extended beyond the church doors). Genuflecting is a damned awkward business, something between a curtsy and an obeisance. Very few people manage it with any style. Most grab the side of the pew, lean heavily upon it as though momentarily stricken with arthritis, and lower their whole body weight on to one knee. They look as though they may never get up again. Others take it at a fast clip as they traverse the aisle: they switch direction like a midfield sweeper, until they are facing the becurtained tabernacle, bob briefly down with the air of a harassed ballerina, and spring back into their cross-church stride.

Communing: going to Communion was a big production. You practically needed a degree to understand and remember everything you were supposed to do – and you did everything you did in emulation of your parents. Deciding exactly when to go, and where to join the queue waiting to receive the Host, was a decision fraught with a million social velleities. It seemed a bit 'common' to rush up to the altar rails the minute the priest started to distribute from the Ciborium (people might think you were desperate). Tagging on right at the end didn't do either; one didn't want to feel or look like an afterthought. No, joining the line of shuffling figures after all the pushy Young Marrieds but before the local tradesmen took their turn, was getting it about right.

You went to the altar rails with eyes cast down, and hands reverently holding each other, as though offering comfort. You looked pensive. Even when you registered the presence, in the other aisle queue, of the divine Mary McCarthy from Arding and Hobbs department store, you dragged your thoughts back to the central mystery of transubstantiation, where they would remain for a matter of seconds. The priest would suddenly loom in front of you, saying, 'The Body of Christ', you'd reply 'Amen', close your eyes, open your mouth, stick out your tongue and receive the Host. The journey back to your seat would be a less convincing performance than the journey to the altar, because one's attempt to look devout, moved and respectful would founder on one's complete inability to find one's seat . . .

Praying: a whole variety of praying styles were available to the faithful. Some Catholic ladies never lost the praying stance they learned at their first Holy Communion – kneeling bolt upright, ramrod back, hands steepled together, eyes closed tight, head lowered until lips meet index fingers. Others would sit canted over in their seats looking sorrowful, like Whistler's mother. Irish men have always had a stance of their own: head bowed, elbow resting on bench in front, hand brought up to cover the eyes. It looks amazingly tragic, like Dan Peggotty a moment after being brought the news about Little Emily and Steerforth. Young English males were generally addicted to the Wally Squat, in which, rather than kneel or sit, one sprawled on one's elbows with one's bottom stuck out to rest against the pew, fatally resembling some unimpressive species of elderly primate.

Candles: there were several reasons for lighting a candle: for a 'special intention', e.g. that you will finally pass chemistry O-level at the third go; for the sake of a soul in Purgatory (this was pure schmaltz, the idea of a solitary candle burning later in the darkened church, like the very epitome of a good deed in a naughty world); for the memory of a loved one; and sometimes just for the hell of it. It was always a uniquely appealing feature of the Catholic Church, that black iron grille covered in thorn-like appendages on which the shilling candles and red votive lights get impaled. It looks like an instrument of torture or death, but is transformed into a gorgeous, flickering, lambent glow of comfort and warmth – an idealised image of the Church itself.

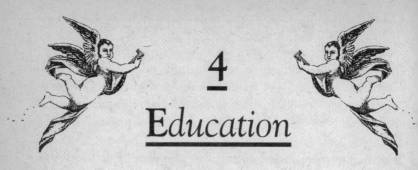

4
Education

WHEN DOES IT START, the long, exhaustive process of induction into the Catholic mysteries? From the first minute your blue eyes focus with any intelligence on the Sacred Heart portrait on the bedroom wall; from the first thoughtless, pyjama-clad incantation of

> *Matthew, Mark, Luke and John,*
> *Bless the bed that I lie on.*
> *Ever this night be at my side*
> *To light and guard, to rule and guide, Amen;*

from the first mention of the terrible word 'disobedience', that's when. Catholic children are expected to be different from the rest. Whatever other children may have been learning at four and five (finger-painting? Suzuki violin?), we were getting the lowdown on morality and virtue.

Virtues at age four? Certainly. From as far back as I can remember, the air was thick with injunctions about how best to lead a truly Catholic life. We were to be modest, self-denying, charitable to others, obedient, optimistic, pure in thought, word and deed, meek, diligent, temperate and humble. It was a rich brew of qualities to balance in a single inchoate temperament while one was still in short trousers; but then learning virtues, learning how to be good, learning especially how to keep out of trouble, was at the very base of our faith.

OBEDIENCE

The first virtue of all was obedience. You were led to believe that hardly anything else mattered so long as you did what you were told. Obedience to parents and teachers, it seemed, was not a matter of choosing to go along with somebody else's orders, or policy, or world view; it was presented as *intrinsically* virtuous. To be obedient was to be Good.

What was Adam's sin? Murder? Rape? Lies? Mutiny? Not at all. It was an open-and-shut case of Disobedience to God's command that he shouldn't eat of the Tree of the Knowledge of Good and Evil.

Where did Satan come from? Why, he was one of God's top angels, promising to go far, when he got too proud of his own fine virtues and refused to accept God's status as his Lord and Master. He refused to *obey* Him any longer, and was in consequence flung into Hell.

Disobedience was the first sin confessed at Confession. In sermons, it was described as a supreme moral triumph to put oneself wholly into the service of another. In Lourdes, a visionary called Father Ryan explained, with tears in his eyes, the *beauty*, the absolute *purity* of perfect obedience – a state in which one could lose the whole grubby sense of ego and be reborn through acquiescence . . .

How long you buy all this depends on the age at which your faith starts to go adrift. I didn't suddenly start being disobedient in my teens, because I didn't want to have to listen to that word any longer. I just started to question things more and more, to refuse to be dammed up by demands for dumb agreement. In later life, it strikes you that the only time *apart* from a Catholic

CATHOLIC RÔLE MODELS

Good	*Not So Good*
Our Lady	Eva Peron
Mother Teresa of Calcutta	Marilyn Monroe
	Torquemada
St Thérèse of Lisieux	Mussolini
Grace Kelly	James Joyce
President Kennedy	Madonna
Joan of Arc	Myra Hindley
Bing Crosby	Johnny Rotten
St Bernadette	Marianne Faithfull
Pat O'Brien	John McEnroe
Malcolm Muggeridge	Terry Wogan
Lord Longford	Peter Sutcliffe
Shirley Williams	Edna O'Brien
Graham Greene	Frank Sinatra
Hilaire Belloc	Jackie Onassis
Victoria Gillick	Dean Martin
St Thomas Aquinas	Princess Michael
St Thomas More	Anne Diamond
Bruce Kent	Brendan Behan
Matt Talbot	

childhood that the words 'obedient' and 'disobedient' are ever
used is in relation to the training of dogs.

THE CATECHISM

Catholic doctrine doesn't proceed from some general religious
premise and move by logical steps into more specific areas of
debate. It starts with the blunt, brain-pounding dictates of the
Catechism. ('The book that's had the greatest influence on my
life, and still the most terrifying book I've read, is the Catholic
catechism': Alan Bleasdale.) Once known as 'the penny Catechism', this remarkable document is still (now forty pence) a
bestseller in churches and Catholic Truth Society bookshops
and – despite many recent revisions – still carries the proud
legend on its cover:

**Approved by the Archbishops and Bishops
of England and Wales,
and directed to be used
in all their dioceses.**

Here is where the Catholic education begins. Learn this, they
said, and you'll never again question your betters about the faith.
All the answers are contained herein. In fact we did not have to
learn by heart every one of the 370 questions and answers – we
were led instead to concentrate on the sections on 'faith', 'the
Commandments' and 'the sacraments'. Nonetheless, fear drove
many to learn the whole thing by rote, including the prayers in
the Appendix and the Imprimatur from Cardinal Heenan on the
flyleaf: it was the tinies' equivalent of learning the Highway
Code off by heart, in anticipation of a particularly stiff and
perverse test examiner.

We were tested regularly. Failure to trot out the correct

wording was an offence regarded with an unusually baleful eye.
Whereas a similar failure to recall your French irregular verbs or
lists of the dates of monarchical births might be greeted with
sarcasm or accusations of indolence, the Catechism was different. It was intrinsically important and deserving of greater
respect: if you didn't know it as you should, you were guilty of a
moral flaw, an ethical backslide, a failure of taste. It felt as
though you were only an approximation of a human being while
you struggled to digest its seventy-odd pages, as though you were
only slowly growing towards some minimum level of decency as
you gradually digested its hectoring creed.

The whole document of interrogation and reply is divided into
several sections. After the most fundamental enquiries of all –
'**Who made me? What must you do to save your soul?**' – it
slowly investigates every phrase in the Apostles' Creed, a
recitation of faith that begins, 'I believe in God the Father
Almighty, Creator of Heaven and Earth', and expresses a belief
in the death and Resurrection of Christ. The section on faith
switches to hope and the Catholic's dwindling expectation that
he'll be saved in spite of everything he's done wrong: this is
where you learn that you can do nothing directly to save yourself,
but can hope to increase your stock of sacramental grace through
devoted prayer and going to the sacraments.

What the Ten Commandments 'expressly' forbid is then
carefully teased out (see Chapter 3) until the original Commandments have all but disappeared: '**What sins**,' asks the Catechism,
'**commonly lead to the breaking of the sixth and ninth commandments?**' (That is, the two concerned with sexual matters.)
'The sins that commonly lead to the breaking of the sixth and
ninth commandments,' comes the reply, 'are gluttony, drunken-
ness and intemperance and also idleness, bad company and the
neglect of prayer.' Clearly this is nonsense – lust is far more likely
to lead to sexual jiggery-pokery than, say, gluttony. But that's

what the Commandments are able to tell us: the Catholic Commandments make their own rules.

They are followed by the 'Commandments of the Church', which are brief and straightforward: you had to attend Mass on Sundays and Holydays of Obligation whenever they fell, Confession and Communion at least once a year. You couldn't marry a non-Catholic without a great fuss – and you were expected to contribute to the upkeep of the church. The Catechism then ends in a flurry of virtues, vices, definitions of sin and 'the Christian's Rule of Life', portraying Jesus Christ as a rôle-model and counselling self-denial.

The oddest thing about this strange little production is its prevailing tone. Throughout all the questions and answers, the voice mostly operates at a pitch of pooh-poohing haughtiness, of slightly incredulous, how-could-you-be-so-stupid prissiness, of inarguable righteousness. Though the prime function of the Catechism was to inform about the fundamentals of Christian doctrine, as interpreted by the Catholic Church, it seemed unable to resist a sly dig there, a brief burst of rant there.

How do we expose ourselves to the danger of losing our Faith?

We expose ourselves to the danger of losing our Faith by neglecting our spiritual duties, reading bad books, going to non-Catholic schools.

Note the subtlety of the warning. Anyone else would reply that the likelihood of one's losing one's faith was in direct proportion to the strength of one's initial conviction. But the Catechism will not deal in such individualism. Stick to the ritual they say, don't read, and lay off the opposition . . .

Sometimes it would boldly enquire how we can 'prove' the unprovable, answering itself by ducking the question completely, thus:

How do you prove that there is a Purgatory?
I prove that there is a Purgatory from the constant teaching
of the Church; and from the doctrine of Holy Scripture, which
declares that God will render to every man according to his
works; that nothing defiled shall enter Heaven; and that some
will be saved 'yet so as by fire'.

You begin to feel you're operating on a closed circuit: according
to this, you can prove that a metaphysical proposition really
exists because the Church that invented the concept continues
to say it's true. Provided Holy Scripture has sanctioned it, it's as
good as built. One more example. **'Can the Church err in what
it teaches?** No, the Church cannot err,' says the Catechism,
patiently. But **How do you know?** comes the question. The
answer is a burst of rhetoric, of considerable power and beauty, in
which the would-be objectivity of the question is soon swamped:

I know the Church cannot err in what she teaches because
Christ promised that the gates of hell should never prevail
against his Church; that the Holy Spirit should teach her all
things; and that he himself would be with her all days, even to
the consummation of the world.

A strange, contradictory to-ing and fro-ing of the physical and
the spiritual characterises much of the book. Take for example
the Apostles' Creed, where God is defined as 'the supreme Spirit,
who alone exists of himself and is infinite in all perfections', a
burst of self-defining metaphysics that would baffle the smartest
seven-year-old sceptic. But what is remarkable is the physicality
with which the Catechism thereafter represents the mysteries of
religion:

Why is God called the Creator of heaven and earth?
God is called 'Creator of heaven and earth' because he made heaven and earth, and all things, out of nothing, by his word.

Had God any beginning?
God had no beginning; he always was, he is, and he always will be.

Where is God?
God is everywhere.

Does God know and see all things?
God knows and sees all things, even our most secret thoughts.

Has God any body?
God has no body; he is a spirit.

I can still feel the tug of anti-climax that accompanied the last of these replies. Once you've had that litanic burst of divine qualifications – making God into, in turn, a magical illusionist, a Time Traveller, an immortal, a Total Surveillance Facility, a Man With X-Ray Eyes, plus a combined psychiatrist and detective (to worm out those secret thoughts) – the last thing you want is for him to turn into a mere doctrinal construct. But the Catechism was always long on declaration and short on explanation.

The Holy Trinity passes by in a blur of meaningless definitions ('**How many natures are there in Jesus Christ?** There are two natures in Jesus Christ, the nature of God and the nature of man.' '**Is there only one Person in Jesus Christ?** There is only one Person in Jesus Christ, which is the Person of God the Son.') before settling back, in obvious relief, to the physical details of the Nativity, the Passion and Christ's return from the dead.

What captures the imagination throughout is the constant
juggling between body and soul, flesh and spirit, Christ and God.
While we were ostensibly enquiring into the ultimate, ineffable
mystery of life, namely the identity of God, the foreground was
full of vivid detail, metaphorical certainly, but real as sixpence to
the average, cowed small boy.

The Catechism professed to disparage those crass enough to
take it all literally ('**What do you mean by the words "is seated
at the right hand of God the Father Almighty"?** I do not mean
that God the Father has hands, for he is a spirit; but I mean that
Christ, as God, is equal to the Father and, as man, is in the
highest place in heaven.'). But at every turn it gave us pictures,
drew us appalling diagrams, re-apprehended the real world for us,
to make it the manor of a strange, tyrannical being, who watched
from a throne on the sidelines like some absentee umpire, who
would eventually come shambling onto the pitch at the least
convenient moment and dish out summary punishments. How
would you have felt, aged seven, to read:

When will Christ come again?
Christ will come again from Heaven at the last day, to judge
all mankind.
What are the things Christ will judge?
Christ will judge our thoughts, words, works, and omissions.
What will Christ say to the wicked?
Christ will say to the wicked: 'Depart from me, ye cursed, into
everlasting fire, which was prepared for the devil and his angels.'

Even the concluding section, The Christian's Daily Exercise,
with its scoutmasterly advice as to everyday etiquette, was filled
with veiled threats. It suggested one's day should be filled with
prayers from the moment of awakening and studded thereafter
with meditation ('especially on the four last things, and the Life

and Passion of our Blessed Lord') with moderation, with good books ('such as the Holy Gospels, the Lives of the Saints and other spiritual works') with frequent calls to God to save one from sin, with stoicism when faced with pain or privation . . .

And at the end of each day, what should you do? Why, 'After my night prayers I should observe due modesty in going to bed; occupy myself with the thoughts of death; and endeavour to compose myself to rest at the foot of the Cross, and give my last thoughts to my crucified Saviour.' That's the last question and answer in the Catechism: a chilly sign-off.

CATHOLIC HYMNS – THE TOP TEN

Ave Maria
Special favourite of Lourdes pilgrims, but sung at weddings and funerals, May processions and the occasional benediction. Astonishingly dull chorus.

God Bless Our Pope
Big Assembly Hall number, sung (for inscrutable reasons) at end of school term. A vote of confidence in the Boss. Unusually vivid lyric and irresistible hook:

> 'Full in the panting heart of Rome
> Beneath the Apostles' crowning dome,
> From pilgrims' lips that kiss the ground
> Breathes in all tongues one only sound –
> God Bless our Pope', etc.

Just for Today

Childishly simple request that the singer be granted the grace of total self-abnegation:

> 'Let me be slow to do my will/Prompt to obey.
> Teach me to mortify my flesh/Sweet Lord today.
> Let me no wrong or idle word/Unthinking say.
> Set thou a seal upon my lips/Just for today.'

Though it stuck in the throats of the hooligan element, this craven little ditty proved immensely popular with the middle-aged faithful.

Faith of Our Fathers

A rousing, cheery, football-crowd yodel ('Fai-haith of our Fa-ha-theh-hers holy faith/We will be true to thee till death') confirming the congregation's adherence to this and no other religion. An espousing of traditionalism that sounds like the swearing-in of a new recruit. The Family of Man meets the Army of the Lord. Great fun.

Sweet Sacrament Divine

A gorgeous hymn, slow, languorous, rather sensual, much liked by the elderly sopranos in the front pews. The titular sacrament (which presumably refers to the Blessed Sacrament of Christ in the tabernacle) comes through the fall of verses to suggest a final haven of equilibrium, a guarantee of comfort and rest: ►

'Sweet sacrament of peace
Dear home of every heart.
Where restless yearnings cease
And sorrows all depart.
Where in thine ear all trustfully
We tell our tale of misery
Sweet sacrament of peace'.

I'll Sing a Hymn to Mary

The children's favourite, the natural stand-by of First
Holy Communions and Queen of the May extrava-
ganzas. As twee as Little Bo-Peep, but without its
intellectual rigour.

Lord of the Dance

Very bouncy folk song by Jeremy Taylor, in which
Christ describes his activities on earth as dances. This
was the song that convinced Mary O'Hara she would be
better off singing than staying in a convent. Extremely
zippy chorus (which you can dance to).

Star of the Sea

A tribute to the Virgin Mary. The simplest imaginable
tune, but lyrically charged with emotion. Done well, it
can be unbearably moving:

'He gazed on Thy soul; it was spotless and fair
For the Empire of sin, it had never been there.
None ever had owned Thee, dear Mother, but He
And He loved Thy clear shining sweet Star of the Sea'. ►

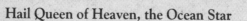

Hail Queen of Heaven, the Ocean Star
Why the Blessed Virgin should be characterised so often as a kind of signal flare for distressed mariners is a mystery. But this is another beautiful hymn that offers an obscure kind of comfort through your life. The final line of the chorus – 'Pray for the wanderer, pray for me' – is a real tear-jerker.

Benedictus Qui Venit
A favourite procession hymn. The sentence 'Blessed is he who comes in the name of the Lord' repeated several times (in Latin). When you finally get to the Hosannas at the end, you feel like cheering. Mostly the tune is murmured rather than sung, a meditation rather than a performance.

The American equivalent, known as the Baltimore Catechism, used to provide several enthralling examples of Catholic problem-solving. Apart from the unlikely Christian names with which the dramatis personae were saddled, there's an air of high camp righteousness about their view of morality. Here are a few examples taken from the 1943 version:

Jonas, a Catholic, has been keeping company with Rania, the daughter of a Protestant minister in the neighbouring town. In three weeks, he plans to be married. Both of his parents are still ignorant of the whole affair. Has Jonas acted correctly towards them? Explain your answer.

(Now you might think that Jonas's socio-sexual arrangements

are his own affair. But when you discover his intended is a Protestant (thus putting the whole family's faith under assault) and a minister's daughter (very hard to argue with Prod ministers) and from the next town (God! *that* bunch) and it's clear the parents must be encouraged to step in.)

Giles is murdered by a Communist just as he leaves the church after his confession. Giles has been away from the Church for twenty-eight years. He just about satisfied the requirements for a good Confession, having only imperfect contrition, aroused during this week's mission. The Communist demanded to know if Giles was a Catholic, threatening to kill him if he was. Fearlessly Giles said, 'Yes, thank God and His Blessed Mother, I am! And proud of it!' Did Giles go immediately to Heaven as he expired on the church steps, or did he go to Purgatory for a while? Give a reason for your answer.

(Well, gosh. How gratifying to have before you, for once, the ground rules for becoming a martyr. Note the throwaway opening ('murdered by a Communist') as though such a conflict happened every day. Marvel at the allegedly limited perfection of Giles's soul, following his first confession for twenty-eight years, which yet prompts him to utterances at which Fotherington-Thomas himself would balk. For anyone less disposed to become a martyr, this little tale illustrates precisely how *not* to address a homicidal Pinko . . .)

The night before her wedding, Viola is so thoroughly concerned with her appearance and her appointment at the hairdresser's that she completely forgets to go to Confession. Unhappily, she is in mortal sin at the time of the ceremony, but she doesn't realise it until after the honeymoon. Now she is greatly upset about the whole matter and does not want to risk her salvation. Was her marriage sacrilegious? Is she really married? Add a reason to both answers.

(Tough on Viola. Marriage and honeymoon over, the main impressions of her earliest days of marriage are of eternal damnation. Note the dubiousness of her being 'in mortal sin' without realising it, even though an important criterion of a sin *being* 'mortal' is that it is wholly willed and volitional. Is she really married, since she forgot to repent for a sin she didn't know she'd committed? Is she hell.)

Oddly, there's an undercurrent of sex beneath this enquiry that perhaps explains the snooty tone. A subsequent question confirms this impression:

If Viola had died suddenly on her honeymoon, would that mortal sin on her soul as she marched up the aisle to the altar have been the cause of her damnation? (*Marched up the aisle,* eh? Poor, damned Viola.)

Muriel, an office worker, is a girl of angelic purity. Many of her associates, even Catholics among them, have vile tongues and still viler imaginations. Muriel never joins in their obscene conversations, and pays no attention to the offensive remarks that are hurled at her from time to time. Even those who pass such indelicate remarks secretly admire the girl's courage. Do you think the sacrament of confirmation that she received years ago is helping her? Is she co-operating with the Holy Ghost? Add a short explanation to your answer.

(One can only speculate about the 'office' where poor Muriel is working. The Houses of Parliament? The *Daily Mirror*? The National Union of Dockers? What is she doing there? Was she, perhaps, taken on *because* of her angelic purity, to provide a good example to the others? Does she know that her interlocutors secretly admire her? How does she know it if she never talks to any of them? Wouldn't *you* like to be Muriel?)

Flora, a member of the Book-of-the-Month Club, reads each book as it is delivered to her home. Some of these books are most unfavourably reviewed by our Catholic publications as

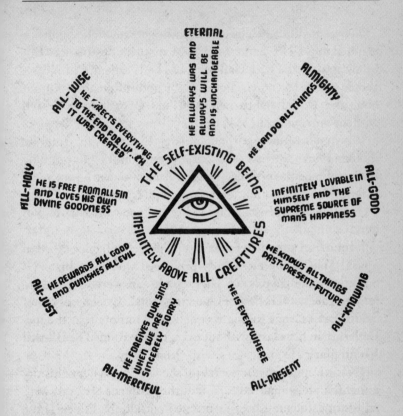

THE SELF-EXISTING BEING

INFINITELY ABOVE ALL CREATURES

ETERNAL
HE ALWAYS WAS AND ALWAYS WILL BE AND IS UNCHANGEABLE

ALMIGHTY
HE CAN DO ALL THINGS

ALL-GOOD
INFINITELY LOVABLE IN HIMSELF AND THE SUPREME SOURCE OF MAN'S HAPPINESS

ALL-KNOWING
HE KNOWS ALL THINGS PAST-PRESENT-FUTURE

ALL-PRESENT
HE IS EVERYWHERE

ALL-MERCIFUL
HE FORGIVES OUR SINS WHEN WE ARE SINCERELY SORRY

ALL-JUST
HE REWARDS ALL GOOD AND PUNISHES ALL EVIL

ALL-HOLY
HE IS FREE FROM ALL SIN AND LOVES HIS OWN DIVINE GOODNESS

ALL-WISE
HE DIRECTS EVERYTHING TO THE END FOR WHICH IT WAS CREATED

endangering faith and morals. Advise Flora as to whether or not she should renew her membership in the club.

(That seems fairly cut and dried, doesn't it? The Church says you shouldn't read what they don't like, so you instantly cancel your subscription and, by implicit extension, stop reading anything not wholly approved of. But what about all the other monthly choices about which the Church has no opinion – is it right that you should be reading them too? And is your faith so tenuous that reading the kind of stuff sent you by a commercial book club will destroy it? For heaven's sake, Flora, lay off the series called 'Books That Have Changed Man's Thinking'. . .)

George is riding in a bus. His mother is very sick. George is inspired to pray for her as he rides along to his destination. But he stops after the first Hail Mary, as he is ashamed of having people see his lips move in prayer. He noticed a man looking at him, and he felt embarrassed. Could George have prayed without moving his lips? Why?

(Can George *think* without moving his lips? But really he shouldn't have worried. The other people on the bus probably had no idea he was praying. They probably assumed he was nuts, took him for a street mutterer, a drunk, a bag-person. All, that is, but the staring man, and God only knows what he had in mind . . .)

Daphne, a Catholic teacher in a public school, once asked in a test, 'Who is the most truly privileged woman in history?' Some of the pupils in her grade answered 'Florence Nightingale', others 'Mary, Queen of Scots', 'Queen Isabella of Spain' and so on. Daphne was delighted to note that the five Catholics in her class, without exception, wrote, 'The Blessed Virgin Mary'. Do you agree with them? Why?

(What Daphne might ponder, if she were a teacher of history rather than religious studies, is that the existence of the BVM as an historical figure is not mentioned outside the Bible. Those who take the Bible as the revealed word of God will argue its status as, ipso facto, an historical document. Others will think the two are quite distinct and that Daphne seems disposed to teach her class historical untruths . . . Anyway, what kind of students could consider that Mary Queen of Scots – consecutively deserted, betrayed, incarcerated and beheaded – had a privileged existence?)

Fidelis, Guy and Malachy are Catholic boys in the sixth grade. They were asked to list five favourite movie actors and five favourite movie actresses. In all, they submitted eighteen different names, all three agreeing on only six. Of their eighteen heroes and heroines, ten are persons who have been married, divorced and remarried, some of them several times and one of them five times. What conclusion do you draw about the wisdom of picking your ideals, your heroes and heroines, from moviedom? State your conclusion in three short sentences.

(Okay, then. 1 Actors have more fun than schoolboys. 2 Fans care as much about the marital shenanigans of actors as about their religious orientation. 3 Whose early life is it safe to take as a rôle-model? St Augustine? Saul?)

PRACTICAL CATACHETICS

It's no great coincidence that the word 'Jesuit' gets itself defined in the *Oxford English Dictionary* as '(derog. archaic) dissembling person, equivocator'. Catholic education was full of ambiguity, moral dilemma, knife-edge debate, attitudinising, argument and falsehood. In true Socratic manner, we were led to consider impossible moral positions and defend our response to them. Every inch of ethical high ground captured was rapidly invaded by a dozen counter-arguments.

I remember at nine being asked to consider the morality of suicide as being a lesser evil than the manslaughter of my fellow men. It was a tall order for a pacifist not yet in long trousers.

'Take this case, Walsh,' the headmaster said grandly. 'You are a special agent in Occupied France in wartime. You are carrying no documents, but you know some vital information about the movements of our troops that you must impart to the Resistance movement.

'Your commanding officer wishes you luck and says: "One last thing, Walsh. In the event of your being captured, it's out of the question that you should submit to interrogation. They're sophisticated torturers, they'll get everything out of you in the end; they will thus be able to anticipate the invasion and huge numbers of our allies will be killed. So if you're captured, take one of these little blue pills, and it'll take care of the problem. Much better that one man should be lost than a whole invading force . . ."

'Now, Walsh, is he right?' the Head gravely asked his quaking recruit. 'Are you justified in killing yourself in order to save the lives of others? Is it still a sin? Can it be forgiven? If it's a mortal sin, you'll go to Hell when you kill yourself. If you don't commit that sin, you'll be responsible for the lives of all those others. You think the Lord will look kindly on that?'

These thorny problems could take up an entire RE lesson, as we wrestled with large concepts of honour, duty, suicide, extinction, torture, murder and similar delights. The answer, invariably, was, 'You would have to explain frankly that, being a Catholic in an irreconcilable dilemma, you must decline such a mission.' But weren't you supposed to do what you were told in the wartime army? Didn't obedience to your commanding officer come into it?

Other Jesuit scenarios concerned Occasions of Sin – what they were, how you got into them, and how you found a way out. The trouble was, these wicked Occasions – though described with distaste in the stern ascetic tones of a lean Jesuit in a shiny soutane – always sounded like out-takes from some spectacular fantasy. My favourite was like an advertisement for coconut chocolate. It concerned a deserted beach. The hot Mediterranean sand. The sun-bleached hair of your young woman companion. The essential innocence of your proximity. The interesting book you're reading (probably St Thomas Aquinas) in companionable silence on a beach mat.

Now for the problem. The girl you're with sits up and removes her brassière, in order to toast her back without leaving strap marks. What do you do? To go on reading a book would be to

disregard her sin of immodesty. To harangue her on the subject
would be unproductive. To indulge in a simple exchange of
views would only embroil you further in disgraceful (and
irrelevant) reflections as to what the rest of her looked like . . .
And so forth. The answer to the question was simple – you
should get up and depart (somewhere, anywhere) as soon as
possible, to avoid remaining any longer in a situation that was
bound to lead to sins of thought, word or deed.

We all sat, I'm afraid, in rapt silence through this one,
wondering if the day would ever come when some girl . . . It was
a tough one to argue. Was there no alternative to just Going
Away, we asked with a desperate note of hope in our voices.
Couldn't you just – y'know – stick around and talk about the
example set by the Apostles and saints, who would never forget
themselves in such a way? We pleaded in vain. As with suicide
missions, topless sunbathing was to be dealt with by the only
action the Church appeared to sanction – pusillanimous retreat,
craven non-involvement.

Other protracted discussions of the Catechism in action dealt
with less earth-shaking concepts than sex and death. These, for
instance:

Fasting What happened if you rendered yourself faint and
inattentive at Mass through deprivation? (Have some water,
which is okay any time.) Did chewing gum count as 'solid food'?
(Yes, until such time as the sugar content had effectively
departed.)

Sunday Mass If you were on safari in some foreign clime, just
how badly off (twelve miles from HQ? bearers dying of exposure?
horses lame? Gatling jammed? no map?) did you need to be
before you could be sure of not being penalised for missing
Mass?

Bearing False Witness Against Your Neighbour   The essential distinction between calumny (when you utter hurtful falsehoods about someone) and detraction (when you utter hurtful truths, that should be kept quiet, about someone). Were white lies sinful, or were they ways of avoiding the sin of detraction as much as avoiding the truth?

The Sacraments   When was a layman allowed to administer them? We were offered a series of vignettes identical to the more secular 'What would you do?' page in the *Lion* comic. The answers were striking. Anyone could baptise a baby if there were fears for its health; a loving couple notionally stranded on a desert island without a priest and thus stuck in a near-permanent Occasion of Sin (for where could either of them depart to?) were reassured that they could still marry – in every wedding the participants perform the ceremony for each other. But the most extreme case was Confession. Should you find a dying person unconscious by the side of the road, you were encouraged to say an Act of Contrition into his ear, in the hope that his final sins would be forgiven. This was more a proxy Confession than a ventriloquial stratagem by which to fool the Holy Ghost.

Secrets   If sworn to secrecy by a friend who has committed a sin (one presumably of no interest to the Metropolitan Police) and had no intention of confessing it, had you a duty to grass to a priest (since you were now an accessory after the fact) or, by doing nothing, to implicitly condone the sin?

Parents   Are you obliged to 'honour thy father and thy mother' if what they require you to do might turn out to be morally dubious? Do you defer more to the law or the family? Can you buy your father cigarettes, as he asks you to, if you're under sixteen (and therefore legally debarred) but look old enough to get away with it?

Vows   You are in dead trouble, and tell the Lord (sincerely at the time) that if he gets you out of this jam, you will perform some spectacular activity – spend the rest of your life with Mother Teresa of Calcutta, build a marble tabernacle, make a pilgrimage to Jerusalem, give away half your future salary to the poor. Things work out unexpectedly well, but common sense tells you it is quite impossible to fulfil your side of the bargain. Will the Lord exact a terrible revenge? Is there anything you can do as an alternative? (The answer's Yes; it's surprising how negotiable Divine Deals turn out to be.)

THE CATHOLIC DIET

The Catholic diet was governed by just two considerations: fasting and abstinence. Both are now gone, but in their day were taken as seriously as the examining of conscience.

Fasting
There was a time when you couldn't eat anything at all on the day you were to receive Communion; nil by mouth from midnight to altar rails. Then the Church relented (since some people could attend only the 6.30 p.m. Mass and receive the sacrament then) and made it a three-hour embargo, to ensure the digestive tracts were well and truly cleansed. Then they made it one hour, which was nonsensical: it was virtually impossible to eat anything less than an hour before receiving the Host.

Fasting was still expected on Good Friday. It didn't mean eating nothing. You were allowed two tiny snacks in the morning and evening, and 'a collation', whatever was meant by that charmingly Jane Austen-ish phrase, around lunchtime. Some Catholics made up their own rules. My father, for instance, decided it was all a matter of the weight of food you were considering consuming. I remember finding him in the kitchen, one Good Friday, solemnly weighing an egg he was thinking of boiling, to make sure it was less than three ounces, the minimum weight he deemed a Proper Meal should be . . .

Abstinence

There was no absolute law that said you had to eat fish on Friday. All that was required was that you kept off red meat, in celebration of Christ's death on a Friday. A rice salad, a spinach quiche, would have done just as well. But by another of those anonymous protocols the Church spreads without realising it, everybody went for fish: herring, haddock, fillet of whiting, cod in batter, halibut in breadcrumbs. It was wonderful. Without the Church's directive, I doubt whether many of us would have tasted a fish lunch before our teens. Mashed potato, a few peas, tomato ketchup, a glass of milk and a chunk of poached turbot with mushrooms – that was the taste of Catholicism once a week. It seemed a great luxury, and one of the Church's more sensible rulings.

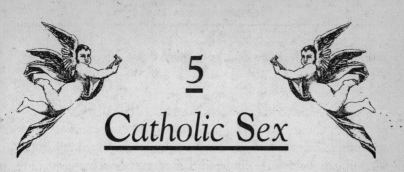

5
Catholic Sex

'WHEN WE WERE CHILDREN, words were coloured,' wrote Louis MacNeice, a Belfast Protestant bishop's son. 'Harlot and murder were dark purple . . .' In a Catholic childhood, the episcopal purple covered every form of sexual activity with a stain of sin. Doing it, talking about it, thinking about it, confusedly wondering about it . . . they instantly involved the hapless, floundering adolescent in a miasma of wrong-doing.

We grew up with a steely conviction, reinforced by each passing day, that every remotely attractive facet of human love was tinged with Hell.

People kissing on television, couples canoodling in the park, cleavages in the newspapers, call-girl scandals in parliament, 'I Can't Get No Satisfaction' on the radio, mini-skirts, Dusty Springfield's kohl-drenched eyes, Mary Quant's pubic-hair locket, *Titbits* in the bike shed, erections in the bath, parties with snogging rooms, rumours in the chemistry lab that girls bled copiously every time you . . . 'Then I Kissed Her' by the Beach Boys, 'Let's Spend the Night Together' by the Stones, 'Pictures of Lily' by The Who – the sense-data of the early sixties will be forever connected, for my classmates, not just with the discovery of sex but with the instant knowledge that everything about it, everything on this list, was Wrong.

CENSORSHIP AND THE DICTIONARY

It started earlier, with discreet forms of censorship. I remember finding that whole sections had been scissored out of the evening paper because they contained things (usually some clucking denunciation of the Permissive Society, complete with graphic examples) considered unsuitable for the young papist's eyes.

Discovering a story that the body of a pregnant woman had been found washed on to the Folkstone shore, I asked my mother what 'pregnant' meant. The response was electrifying. 'Where did you hear that word?' she demanded. I was merely an inquisitive ten-year-old, who might with as much interest have asked the meaning of 'nationalistic' or 'pantechnicon': but it threw my poor parent into such a lather of uncertainty, I resolved never to do it again. The message got through, though – pregnancy as a subject was off-limits to good boys.

Because our main access to the *terra incognita* of sex was through the printed page, our mentors' efforts to retard our education in these matters became ever more insistent. The dictionary, the film magazine, the biology textbook, the novels of Ian Fleming, the new breed of mildly lubricious magazines for teenage girls (*Honey*, *19*, *Petticoat*) were all minefields of salaciousness. The magazines were finally rumbled by a nosey group of Catholic parents, and banned from young Catholic bedrooms. The magazines (*Photoplay* was the best, with its invariable diet of pneumatic, bikinied lovelies to accompany its perfunctory reviews) were discovered in one's satchel and torn asunder. The textbooks, being legitimate aids to academic study, were harder to censor, but their perusal was monitored with hawk-like vigilance.

You'd think the dictionary would be exempt from such concerns. Not at all. If you were caught looking up, say, 'rape' or 'sodomy' in the *Shorter Oxford*, there was trouble of a particularly awful kind: you'd be subjected to a little chat – that is, a half-hour of cringe-making discussion which so triumphantly skirted round the essential facts that you were left no wiser.

Thus, trying to ascertain the meaning of 'prostitute', you would check the family's *Chambers Twentieth Century Lexicon*, to be confronted there with 'Prostitute, n., a whore'. Great. So you looked up 'whore', to be enlightened by the definition 'Whore, n., a harlot' . . . This loop of unhelpful explanations continued through strumpet, tart, *fille de joie*, streetwalker, woman of straw and perhaps a dozen others. I was tantalised beyond endurance. So I took the only other course of action and asked the allegedly raffish Aunt Maureen, who happened to be staying.

'Auntie, what's a prostitute?'

She turned pale and suggested I asked my mother such things.

'But Auntie, don't you know?' I insisted, implicitly suggesting that she possessed more inside knowledge than she should have done.

'Yes of course I do,' she snapped, after which she could do little except spill the beans.

But what picture of a prostitute did I take away with me? Somebody who wore lipstick, lots of lipstick, who got up at three in the afternoon, went around smothered in oodles of cheap scent, wore a feather boa; and there was something about accepting drinks from men in bars, laughing raucously, eventually crying into her gin and having a baby which she wouldn't care for. It all sounded rather jolly. Prostitutes (the baby apart – it seemed a wholly irrelevant refinement) were clearly good sports who broke the rules from time to time. The one thing missing from Aunt Maureen's impressionistic survey was any sense of real wrong-doing and any sense of sin (beyond a rather risqué way with clothes). Instead there was a lot of clucking disapproval with a prostitute-shaped gap in the middle where the information should have been.

When I was found looking up 'rape' ('to assault sexually' the *Chambers* helpfully construed) the lengthy and elaborate definition I received from another mature and earnest female relation, bent on explaining the awfulness of the sin, was full of incidental details: the horrible man lying in wait behind bushes (Clapham Common was deemed the likeliest place), the tea-cloth used for strangling the victim, the innocence of the poor girl, the likelihood of a prison sentence. The whole activity came across as a form of street robbery, no more. Once again, a thick fog of details came down from the grown-up Catholic sky and obliterated the significance of the activity, and the sin.

Since both my parents were medical people, the house was crammed with revoltingly illustrated manuals of forensic science and midwifery, a distressingly graphic flood of quasi-biological information quite superfluous to my needs. I could have delivered lectures on the incidence of super-orbital lesions in murder victims or pyloric stenosis in infants, but of girls' bodies and what exactly you were supposed to do with or to them, I remained in the dark.

Because the prevailing mood of the sixties was liberationist, experimental, iconoclastic and generally tolerant of other people's sillier quirks (their clothes, their politics, their mantras), the Catholic education system found itself under siege. The more they insisted on the 'immodesty' of the time, the 'impurity in thought, word and deed' that leapt from every media screen, the more they passed on to the faithful their disgust, the less they were being heeded by the younger believers. The Church was itself in danger of becoming an anachronism, marginalised by the new freedoms of the Age of Aquarius.

We were given new rôle-models to emulate. In the parish magazine, it was explained that mini-skirts weren't necessarily that bad, provided they were worn with decorum, and gave us a picture of Petula Clark, looking leggily modest, to prove it. The charms of Mr Val Doonican as an entertainer were praised at the expense of, say, P.J. Proby, the notorious trouser-splitter. The humour of Tommy Cooper, they ritually said, was the finest around because 'at least he's clean'. Everywhere, old-style decency was shown as confronting new-wave vulgarity and winning. It was a victory for decency rather than excellence, but Catholic consciences tend to find the two inextricably mingled.

SEXUAL ETIQUETTE

Catholic sexual etiquette was a precisely judged matter of not doing anything in a variety of interesting ways. A good while before you'd contemplated any form of sexual congress – when you were still at the stage of having the connection between apples and their pips explained by your mortified father – you ran into an awesome list of what was theoretically available but in practice quite beyond the pale. It went as follows:

Talking
Holding Hands
Kissing
French Kissing
Petting
Heavy Petting
Handling
Intercourse

The miasma of wrong-doing that surrounded this chart of carnality (which we all faithfully wrote down in our religious instruction copybooks, the fountain pens trembling in our thirteen-year-old fingers) initially led us to believe that there was nothing at all you could do with a girl that was free from some taint of sin.

Catholic sex education started in a mist of sentimentality before getting down to business with the Smut List. There was no greater thing in the world, we learned, than human love; it was the greatest gift of God, and we should be profoundly grateful for it. The love of parents for children and vice versa; the love of friends for each other; the love of the faithful for the Lord, and its unimaginably intense reciprocal equivalent. The love between a husband and wife (we all began to sit forward) that strengthened the bond between them for all their lives and united a Catholic family into an even tighter entity. Love is wonderful, they said, perhaps a shade too insistently. *Really* great.

Now about sex (we all sat up straight), that too is wonderful. Sex within marriage is a bond that seals together . . . yes, yes, yes, we thought impatiently, but what about *outside* marriage? A dark strato-cumulus clouded the Jesuit brow. Sex that is not part of a loving relationship sanctioned by God through the sacrament of marriage is a grave sin against Holy Purity. The sixth and ninth Commandments were immediately invoked: immodesty . . . impurity . . . words, looks, actions . . . thought, word or deed . . . alone or with others . . . bad company . . . immodest dress . . . indecent films and books . . .

But why were they considered so bad? What was the big deal? And so it was unfolded, the great mystery of the sexual urge, the great hunger of lust, the tyranny of the endocrinal system. Our natures, we learned, made us uniquely disposed towards sins of impurity. We could (in fact probably would) lose our judgment in the heat of the moment, and be abandoned to lust if we didn't approach the question of sex in a proper light. Behind these words lay an unspoken, barely thinkable, assumption – that if we forgot ourselves regarding God's laws, we would find at least half-willing co-conspirators among the opposite gender.

Sex, then, represented the easiest and fastest way of falling into mortal sin available to the teenager; but a certain enlightenment among the clergy simultaneously dictated that a league table of wrongness was provided. It was up to your conscience to decide where to stop.

Girls began to take on a threatening aspect: all the Mandys and Margarets, the Carols and Janes, the friends of one's sister, the teenage shop-assistants, the strict-looking, bosomless entities that came to school debates, the uniformed little parcels from the convent in their soft felt hats (winter) and straw boaters (summer) – could they really be these explosive repositories of sin, to touch whom would bring about your instantaneous damnation? The very unlikeliness of the idea only increased its fascination.

Once you'd got past the stage of wholesale paranoia (with some of us it lasted well into our teens), and realised that some things at least were allowed, it was time to encounter the eighty-four-trillion-dollar question of How Far Can You Go? It wasn't just a matter of stopping halfway down the list and going for a cold shower. Everything was suspect.

Talking   You think that's innocuous? You had to make sure you weren't consciously and single-mindedly steering the conversation round to matters of scandal, impertinent enquiries ('So tell me, they still make you wear blue serge knickers at that place?'), ingenuous chitchat about the Virgin Birth, quotations from the racier classical poets (especially Byron and, whew, Lord Rochester), heterodox theories about religious matters (trying to explain exactly what was going on in the Ecstasy of St Theresa invariably led to trouble), or invitations to events whose sole purpose was to provide an Occasion of Sin (q.v.).

Holding hands   Fine, with two exceptions. The hands thus conjoined were not supposed to stray towards the coat or (forget it) trouser pocket. And inserting an exploratory tickling middle finger against the palm of the notional beloved was, for some reason, considered unimaginably immodest.

Kissing   The rôle-model for the Catholic snog was a more tender version of the nun's kiss, that lays cheek against cheek and kisses the air. If your lips met, they were to part again as soon as possible, as though the notional beloved were smitten with garlic or radioactivity. The teeth were to be clamped firmly shut throughout.

French kissing   You weren't likely to discover the distinction between this and the above for a few years. As advised by the likes of the agony aunts in the Irish Sunday papers, this was permissible only during a phenomenally long-standing engagement, and only with a full understanding that it might lead to things which were better restrained from the outset. The implication that this comparatively simple act would guarantee you had a raging sexual tigress on your hands within seconds caused generations of boys to sit in silent wonderment for days on end.

Petting   Merely considering this intermediate stage could bead your spotty forehead with perspiration. Its fine distinctions tended to split the female body into several divisions, like the butcher's shop diagram that explode a bullock into edible sections of haunch, collar, neck and intestines.

   Where were the dangerous areas? Elbows were fine. Shoulders, fine. Armpits, fine-ish (but watch it). Ankles, okay I suppose. Knees, highly suspect. Thighs, absolutely out of bounds. Tummy, well all right then (but who do you think you're fooling?). What was there left to pet? Ah yes. The eternal

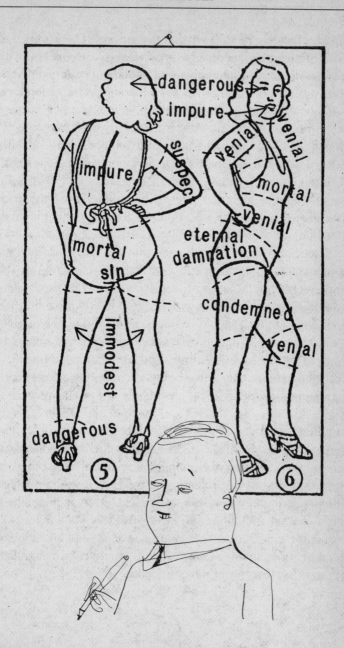

mystery of female breasts was what petting meant. You were not, except in the most guardedly devotional way (and virtually with written permission from the young lady) to clamp your hand round a breast, nor jiggle it up and down, nor twirl it round and round, nor knead it like Plasticine, nor utter any form of compliment or suggestion concerning it. If you brushed lightly against the very edge of the angora jumper, then gallantly declined to pursue the matter, you were doing just about right.

Heavy petting This was the crucial one. As with French Kissing, most of us had no clue how it differed in distinction from its lighter counterpart, only that it was entering very murky water indeed. Gradually it dawned that the Heavy variety was about invading your partner's clothing and clutching at the groin. Worries about just how many centuries in Purgatory were being racked up for you with each pathetic assault on a recalcitrant bra strap would be forgotten in class as one listened to one's associates' man-of-the-world discussions of how they managed to get 'upstairs-inside' and 'downstairs-outside'. At least it brought an answer to the ancient question. *That* – both upstairs and downstairs – was precisely How Far You Went.

Handling This was always left in decently veiled obscurity. The generic name made it sound unwontedly physical, an activity on a par with coal-heaving, operating light machinery or dishonestly passing on stolen property. That it was connected with the genitalia was never made clear. That it might be a matter of what you allowed to be done to you was a revelation lurking some way into the future. That it was an absolute disgrace to oneself, one's family, friends, priests, teachers and all the saints in Heaven was never in doubt.

Intercourse This activity, so wholly out of bounds, so shameful, so unheard-of even among one's most raffish colleagues, was the least discussed. Nobody did it, nor was likely to do it for (we assumed) decades, so it hardly seemed worth the worry. Had we been invited to Do It several times a day, we would, I'm sure, have refused. However allegedly delightful, it was just too overwhelming to contemplate, too embarrassing to anticipate and it meant complete and permanent Hell.

NATURE'S WARNING SIGNAL

For the really puzzled wayfarers in this behavioural minefield, we were patiently told, God had thoughtfully provided a guide, a moral and physical lodestone. If you were going too far with a girl, if the movie you were watching was indeed immodest, if the conversation was becoming sinfully extreme, something weird would start to happen to you. An odd creeping sensation would steal through your bowels and you'd feel as though you were turning to stone. Only one bit of you would be affected, but it was enough of a Sign. It was, announced our old priest with a dramatic pause, 'Nature's warning signal'. As with stress, it was a call to fight or flight – and civilised creatures flee. They put the girl down, make an excuse and leave.

Varying the metaphor, he came up with the brilliant formulation of 'Nature's amber light'. Were you going to screech to a halt, reining in your pantherish, eight-cylinder motor to a meek purr? Or were you a vile and dangerous speed-hog, foolhardy enough to jump the lights and crash straight into the silver juggernaut of the Lord and suffer the consequences? 'What you must ask yourselves,' he suggested helpfully, 'is: "Have I a good reason for carrying on?"'

Erections caused all kinds of terminological problems. When

they weren't being referred to as storm beacons or traffic signals, they were regarded as irresponsible incitements to the sin of self-abuse. They were – not very directly – frowned on by the ninth Commandment, thus: 'The ninth Commandment forbids all wilful consent to impure thoughts and desires, and all wilful pleasure in the irregular motions of the flesh.'

That particular circumlocution was far from helpful. When you came from a household in which 'motions' and 'keeping regular' exclusively referred to the bowels, it was easy to fall into the trap of thinking that the ninth Commandment warned you off diarrhoea. How you could derive pleasure, wilful or not, from such a condition was, we assumed, yet another sacred mystery whose elucidation lay in the future.

JOINING THE BOYS

Naturally we came to wonder if the girls' school taught the same graduated system of sex-by-numbers, and were disappointed to find out they didn't. Instead, a general, fascinating facts-'n'-info talk would be given to the whole school about What Went Where by a visiting social worker clad in an unwelcoming serge suit.

Girls learned about sex in biology lessons – and then it was mainly animal or bird or fish reproduction rather than human. The religious education class threw up one or two items of sexual etiquette, but that was that. Topics that were later (post-*Humanae Vitae* later) to become red-hot were barely referred to. Contraception was simply wrong. The purpose of sex inside marriage was to produce children and that was all; you weren't, as it were, there to enjoy yourselves. So the question of putting the act of procreation to one side in favour of purely recreational sex just didn't arise.

Likewise abortion, in the years before the Abortion Act was passed, was not a topic for discussion. It was considered so disgusting, so clearly out-of-court, that to discuss its rights and wrongs would have been like discussing the torture of small babies. In convents where a schoolgirl got pregnant, abortion was an option that was often gratefully taken by the parents, provided no word of it ever got back to the nuns.

The bottom line for convent girls was the endless pursuit of the Grace of Holy Purity: which meant, essentially, do not be touched, remain a virgin until you are married, and don't talk about it afterwards.

Behind the non-involvement, the non-information, the implications about the number of predators lying in wait, lay the unspoken threat of rampant masculinity. It brought out, in certain girls' schools, some spectacular examples of sexual diplomacy.

A convent friend remembers being told that if she happened to be joining 'a bunch of young people' for a night out in which a car was involved, no good would come of sitting on a male lap. Recognising, though, that social pressure might force her charges to comply with an invitation to share the passenger seat with some priapic lout, she suggested, 'Why not take a book or magazine along to slip under you?' Fair advice – but what book? The E–K telephone directory? (Surely overdoing it.) A copy of *The Tablet*? (Hardly thick enough to be effective.) *Little Women*? *Moby Dick*? The more we considered the problem, the less it yielded.

MARY CRAIG

The old nun who took us for school certificate religion . . . told us more than once that we should not use the word 'body' or think at all about our bodies. For modesty's sake we were

supposed to avert our eyes while bathing. This went deep and I
was already a halfway Manichee when one day our Headmis-
tress summoned the Fifth Form. We had been invited to a dance
that evening run by the local Christian Brothers' Catholic
grammar school. The Head expressed her horror at the discovery that so many of us were going. Good Catholic girls like
ourselves, she shuddered, had no business attending events
where we were likely to be (and I quote) 'pawed by boys'.
Docile though we were, her comments shocked us deeply.
Another of her colleagues had earlier told us that, if we were
asked to dance by a young man, we must first enquire if he was a
Catholic . . .
(From 'Once a Catholic', published in *Why I am Still a Catholic*,
Collins, 1982)

Irish schools had a few helpful words to stop anything going
too far: in a Sligo school, a friend remembers, the following
excellent advice was offered to teenagers in danger from open-air
courtship: 'If a boy takes you home after an evening out, and he
tries to kiss you, make sure you have either a gate – or the
distance of a gate – between you . . .'
Girls in British convents were dissuaded from unconscious
displays of immodesty. Handstands were frowned on. Crossing
one's legs was deemed tarty. (An old Dublin lady once
approached Edna O'Brien in church and said, without preamble,
'Did you not know that every time a young woman crosses her
legs in church, the Virgin Mary blushes?') The advent of tights
was greeted with relief because they were so much less inflam-
matory than stockings and suspenders; in one convent it was
forbidden to run in the corridor because running allowed for
glimpses of the flesh between stocking and knicker, known coyly
as 'smiles'.

WENDY PERRIAM

We were warned off many experiences because they were supposed to be connected to sex. I was told that horse-racing was 'sexually dangerous', and so was dancing. We were told that men's hand were 'dangerous' too. The general impression was that sex was something both dangerous and wicked, and it was on the whole best just to keep away from men. At this point the only men I knew, apart from my father, was our old gardener, and a Polish keep-fit enthusiast.

So when I finally had my first sexual experience, it was a terrible disappointment, a banal and pathetic fumble. After all the terrifying build-up, the talk about it being the most appalling sin you could possible commit . . . I felt there should be more to it. I had imagined it would be darkly wicked and evil.

Girls were advised not to ascend to the upper deck on a bus for fear of boys looking up their skirts and being incited to acts of impurity.

The most famous piece of advice as to the preserving of schoolgirl modesty was that girls should not wear black patent leather shoes – in theory it enabled unusually hawk-eyed lechers to see the reflection of their knickers in the polished instep. This bizarre injunction did exist and was faithfully repeated year after year; but I know not a single ex-schoolboy who ever caught a glimpse of underwear by such fortuitous means, or even realised that it was possible to do so.

The majority of Catholic girls, we later found out, were just as traumatised as we by the darker implications of sex education – the feeling that to have any emotional involvement with the opposite sex which progressed to the realm of physicality was to become instantly compromised. The chief emotion was shame – that one was doing something which, though the result of a natural drive, was gross, dirty, unworthy of your decent home, school and background, and unquestionably sinful to boot. Even tampons were forbidden in a Reading convent in the late sixties (I was told) to 'discourage cheap thrills'. Sanitary pads alone were acceptable.

To some, in hindsight, it was the feeling that an intrusive God was peeping at them, that turned their feelings of guilt into something worse. As a rule of thumb, they were told not to do anything they would be ashamed of their parents seeing or knowing about. In the darkness and solitude of a late-evening clinch, it was possible to forget such considerations (parents are better off not knowing such things), but God would still be watching. However mature you might be, however cool a teenager, that subconscious sense of divine surveillance caught you still, like the little girl who refused to visit the lavatory because she knew that God – the all-seeing – would be watching her having a pee.

Many girls had crushes on young priests who arrived in the convent as part of a mission. To an extent they would be taking their cue from the nuns who fluttered and flapped like bantams when a priest came a-calling; for the rest of the time, their emotional energies were channelled into work or an intense love for the convent cat. Some girls experienced early sexual fantasies about the naked body of Christ on the Cross. Some found the experience of Confession profoundly disturbing, as they knelt, whispering in the dark, confiding their sinfulness to a barely-glimpsed male profile.

Among all these tormented wonderings, boys rarely got a look-in. They were given such a damning press by the convent teachers that no sensible girl would want to look at them. They were represented as vicious, self-seeking, predatory, over-tactile, emotionless, bestial creeps who – if 'allowed' any liberties – would take advantage of you. And it wasn't really their fault, but that of their nature, which made them driven and unstoppable. Whew! Germaine Greer's main beef against her Australian convent was that it made men sound too interesting – feral, passionate, strong-willed – and left a lot of ex-schoolgirls greatly disappointed when the truth became clear.

STORMING THE TABERNACLE

So much for the Catholic line on sex with others. Sex by, with or from oneself was a different, but equally traumatic affair. Masturbation, nocturnal emissions, unexpected engorgements on the upstairs of a bus, were all breaches of Catholic etiquette. They were all regarded with deep suspicion, not because they were grave sins – masturbation from (as it were) a standing start was technically a mortal sin, but had lesser venial forms, while the other two were not sins at all – but because they transgressed one fundamental law of Catholic belief: the belief that 'your body is the tabernacle of the Holy Ghost'. It didn't matter that we had no clue as to what could be meant by this opaque phrase. We got the message soon enough: your body doesn't really belong to you. You are only caretaking it for a higher power. So don't muck about with it.

The 'tabernacle' theory – that your body must be always pure enough to provide a home for the Blessed Sacrament (at Communion) – implied that the whole body was involved in this sacred trust. But because the phrase only seemed to be used (in a condemnatory mode generally) in matters of sex, the two became confused. Suddenly, it seemed, your winkle had turned into the tabernacle of the Holy Ghost.

Alexander Portnoy, the Olympic-standard masturbator of *Portnoy's Complaint*, was of course Jewish, but has several Catholic avatars, similarly hounded by their mothers. A friend remembers how his mother considered making an appointment for him at the Ear, Nose and Throat Clinic because of the volume of paper tissues he was getting through. Another recalls the guilt of his first wet dream: certain that he was abnormal and leaking corruption, he prowled round the house in the morning unable to change the bed-linen (the airing cupboard was locked) and dreading the consequences. Finally he was summoned to his own bedroom. The conversation went:

'What happened to you, James? Were you sick in the night?'

Mumble, mumble, 'No.'

'Well you must have been blowing your nose on the sheet, then.'

Mumble mumble, 'For Heaven's sake, Ma . . .'

'Well I can't think what . . . unless . . .'

'Look, Ma, it happens to everybody—'

'Unless of course all those fine films you've been seeing, and all these great friends of yours with their nice talk . . .'

'Look, it's perfectly natural—'

'Oh, is it indeed? Is it now? I wonder.'

At which point James retired, convinced once again that he was constructed differently from everybody else, given to grosser physical habits than anyone else (and they were his fault, too) and more utterly doomed to perdition, due to sins of impurity, than anybody else in Christendom.

AVERTING THY GAZE

Immoral, impure, immodest . . . how those three words circled the brain like tiny satellites in those days. We weren't sure how they differed in essence from each other, but we assumed they meant much the same thing:

'Immoral' meant something to do with sex, only with a high ethical gloss on it – like befriending a prostitute who was part of a circle of thieves and murderers.

'Impure' meant something to do with sex, only something exclusively physical – it was most used when you were warned off self-abuse or counselled against heavy petting (and just before the words 'your body is the temple of the Holy Ghost' were trotted out once again).

'Immodest' meant something to do with sex, only something *visual* – immodest was the word used about films, books, the Wednesday play, strip shows, Soho, short skirts, cleavages, the whole thing.

The trouble was, there were so many visual distractions around, almost all connected in some degree with sexual imagery, that the Church was hard pressed as to where to start tamping it down. They could confiscate books, but fiercely hated embarking on arguments about whether *Lady Chatterley* was or was not Literature. They had more success with films by denouncing them from the pulpit at Friday Benediction, and giving the impression that half the staff would be waiting outside the Wimbledon Odeon on Saturday after each performance, to see who came out. (In fact, half the films they denounced we couldn't see anyway simply because we hadn't reached the Certificate X age watershed.)

So mostly they left it to our consciences, to Nature's Warning Signal and the paranoia engendered by parental vigilance.

The Church in the forties and fifties, however, had a very strict eye for the morally dubious – not the Vatican, you understand, but the Catholic pressure groups which lobbied Hollywood and threatened to boycott films that didn't pass their rigorous scrutiny. This was no idle threat – the Legion of Decency, at its height, boasted ten million members.

What did they object to? There were six classifications:

AI	▶ Morally unobjectionable for general patronage
AII	▶ Morally unobjectionable for adults and adolescents
AIII	▶ Morally unobjectionable for adults
AIV	▶ Morally unobjectionable for adults (with reservations)

| Class B | ▶ **Morally objectionable in part for all** |
| Class C | ▶ **CONDEMNED** |

Would *anyone* wish to go to a Legion AI-rating movie? Thousands did – they included the Bing Crosby-and-the-nuns bestselling double, *Going My Way* and *The Bells of St Mary's*, *The Sound of Music*, and a number of films that featured either nuns (*The Trouble with Angels*, *The Singing Nun*) or miracles witnessed by visionaries (*Miracle at Lourdes*, *Saint Joan*) or occasionally both (*Song of Bernadette*).

The other three A classifications grudgingly passed the bulk of movies released in the forties and fifties, while waggling a finger at any portrayals of passion or hints of blasphemy. The first Class B (morally objectionable) rating went to *Gone With the Wind*, because of the line, 'Frankly my dear, Ah don't give a damn', and presumably also because of Scarlett O'Hara's astonishingly unscrupulous character. The same fate befell *The Outlaw*, purely (if that's the word) because of the prurient emphasis on Jane Russell's bosom. Wrangles over the Decency rating and the requirements of the censorship lobby held up the film's release for six years.

Other notable victims were Garbo's last film, *Two-Faced Woman* (in which she plays a woman who impersonates her more lively twin sister, in order to win back the husband she is losing to another woman); *A Streetcar Named Desire*, in which the crazed romantic Blanche Dubois (Vivien Leigh) is raped by her revolting brother-in-law (Marlon Brando); and *The Man With the Golden Arm*, in which Frank Sinatra plays a Chicago poker dealer hooked on heroin. The fact that he constantly tries (and finally succeeds) to kick the habit clearly didn't impress the Legion; they found the halfway sympathetic portrayal of Windy City lowlifes morally reprehensible anyway.

The Condemned: Not many films were actually condemned

from the pulpit. In some cases, the Legion of Decency demanded, and got, certain cuts that rendered a movie Class B rather
than the terminal C. The distinction was crucial: Catholics were
told that it was a sin to go and see any Class C movies. Simple as
that.

These were on the black list:

The Miracle. Anna Magnani plays a thick peasant girl who
believes she had immaculately conceived her baby after being
seduced by a shepherd.

The Moon is Blue. Otto Preminger's briefly notorious story
about a liberated girl with a young boyfriend and a middle-aged
lover. The first time the words 'virgin', 'mistress' and 'seduce'
were heard in the cinema.

Baby Doll. Elia Kazan's dark and decadent study of Deep
Southern repressions, in which the sexually inert, thumb-
sucking Carroll Baker is seduced by her violent husband's nasty
rival. *Time* magazine called it 'possibly the dirtiest American-
made motion picture that has ever been legally exhibited'.
Cardinal Spellman of New York thundered its denunciation in
St Patrick's Cathedral.

In the sixties they found many more to condemn (*The
Pawnbroker*, *Blow-Up*, *Who's Afraid of Virginia Woolf*, *Midnight
Cowboy*, *Satyricon*, *Zabriskie Point*, *MASH*, *Carnal Knowledge*,
A Clockwork Orange, *The Last Picture Show*). But the League of
Decency was running out of steam, and being overtaken by the
modern world. In 1980, short of cash and new converts, it passed
away.

THE CATHOLIC BOOKSHELF

Catholics   Brian Moore
Apologia Pro Vita Sua   John Henry Newman
Autobiography of a Soul   St Thérèse of Lisieux
The Path to Rome   Hilaire Belloc
The Innocence of Father Brown   G.K. Chesterton
The Greatest Story Ever Told   Fulton Oursler
The Shoes of the Fisherman   Morris West
The Heart of the Matter   Graham Greene
Brideshead Revisited   Evelyn Waugh
Memories of a Catholic Girlhood   Mary McCarthy
Frost in May   Antonia White
A Portrait of the Artist as a Young Man   James Joyce
For Whom the Bell Tolls   Ernest Hemingway
How Far Can You Go?   David Lodge
The Keys of St Peter   Roger Peyrefitte
Hadrian the Seventh   Fr. Rolfe, Baron Corvo
Holy Pictures   Clare Boylan
The Mandelbaum Gate   Muriel Spark
The Bridge of San Luis Rey   Thornton Wilder
The Small Miracle   Paul Gallico
The Roman Persuastion   Bernard Bergonzi
After Purple   Wendy Perriam
Holy Mother   Gabrielle Donnelly
Seeing Things   Frances Thomas

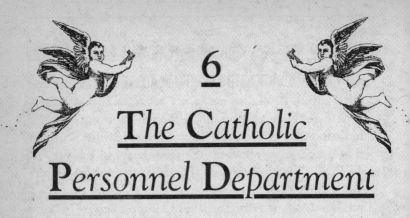

6
The Catholic Personnel Department

THE CATHOLIC CHURCH, in both its spiritual and earthly manifestations, is a more hierarchical and more bureaucratic set-up than any company or government or branch of the armed forces.

THE BOARD OF DIRECTORS

At the head of its megalithic spiritual corporation, the benign, all-seeing, ever-present Chairman is God; by his side – and ostensibly sharing in his divinity, as you find in several well-run multinationals – are Christ the Son of God (celestial nepotism, you see) who acts as a kind of Marketing Director for the Church on earth, and the Holy Ghost, whose functions – apart from impregnating blessed virgins and transmigrating into the shape of a dove every now and then – are wholly inscrutable. He is best thought of as an éminence grise, a shadowy, rarely seen, backroom figure like a management consultant.

WENDY PERRIAM

I felt I had been born into an extended family of saints and guardian angels, as real to me as my relations. I particularly loved St Francis and St Joseph, although there was a saint around for every occasion. I always imagined my guardian angel as a him — he followed me everywhere, so I never felt lonely. When I lost my faith, it was a wrench having to give him up . . .

I was never very keen on the Virgin Mary, I suppose because I was never like her; she seemed so demure, so passive and accepting. I resented her like mad for being so boring, and focused on God instead. I saw him as a glamorous, heroic figure — a film star, like Stewart Grainger, in a suit, smoking a cigarette. The Devil attracted me as a Heathcliffe figure — wild, hairy, madly attractive, probably with a deformed foot. I dreamed of making overtures to the Devil and offering him my soul. I was sure I'd be damned, but I believed in him emotionally. The kind of students I was meeting in those days, with their spots and nervous manners, just couldn't compare with a fallen angel . . .

THE ANGELS

The downstream operatives in Heaven are multitudinous, and cannot sustain the corporate analogy. No one else is needed, after all, in the boardroom besides the chief operatives — there are no budgets, no research and development, no critical path analysis in a place of supreme perfection. The personnel are perhaps best thought of as components of an army. Theoretically they're all soldiers and civil servants combined, but some are grander than others and some have their own personal battalions.

You thought there'd be no competition in Heaven? Well, you'd be half right. No one there thinks of back-stabbing a senior or shafting a pushy newcomer to teach him a lesson. They are all angels, all perfect beings. But, the Catechism used to tell us, there are grades and grades. 'Do all the blessed in Heaven enjoy equal happiness? All the blessed in Heaven do not enjoy equal happiness; those who served God more faithfully and gained more merit will enjoy a proportionately greater happiness.' In the same way, this variously happy breed will find there that among the untold squillions of angels, up to ten orders – I found the names in the *Dictionary of Angels* – can be found (and for God's sake don't mix them up):

Seraphim: you imagine them as immensely tall, pale and ascetic, gliding through vast libraries, dining at High Table and exchanging murmurs of recondite learning.

Cherubim: pink-cheeked, rather immature, sporty, practical jokers, throwers of bread rolls at the celestial banquet.

Thrones: as the name implies, masters of committee agenda, experts at housing problems, will require everything minuted.

Dominions: high-powered diplomats, sticklers for protocol, very grand and condescending pressers of the flesh.

Virtues: impossibly smug goody-goodies, endlessly showing off their merit badges, still holier-than-thou even in Heaven.

Powers: tough bouncer figures, deceased policemen etc., on call in the unlikely event of an 'incident'. Possibly whisky drinkers.

Principalities: conceited hereditary heirs of minor heavenly kingdoms, down on their luck but full of good stories of the old days.

Archangels: authoritarian, school-prefect version of common-or-garden angels, sometimes let out for small civic duties on earth, public announcements etc., cf. Gabriel. There are only seven, each reputedly accompanied by 490,000 lesser angels, an organisational nightmare.

Angels: the rank and file. Most do little except exchange chitchat at the celestial cocktail party, and count their blessings.

Guardian angels: nice, stable, caring, minder-figures. Each new soul is granted a guardian angel, who stands by your bed like a night-light and watches over you while you're asleep. They are always with you, an eternal, non-judgmental friend, losing whom is a wrench as many lapsed Catholics will admit. One imagines them fretting in Heaven over their lost charges: 'He never writes, he never phones, I've been worried sick . . .'

THE VIRGIN MARY

If Jesus Christ ascended to Heaven to sit at the right hand of His Father, God the Father, just what fate befell the Virgin Mary after she was Assumed into Heaven? Does she have a significant rôle to play in the top echelons of Paradise?

Which leads to the key question: how does she get on with, how does she stand in relation to, God the Father? She is the mother of Christ, who is part of the Trinity of Godhead. Also part of the Trinity is God the Father. Mary therefore contrives to be the mother of her child's Father . . .

It's no good. Mary's exact position in the line-up is another mystery denied to mere mortals. But it always led us to suspect that her earthly state was secretly deemed to be all she was good for – that her function as a vessel, by which Christ would assume human shape, was her only point; and after she had fulfilled this rôle, there was nothing for her except tears and exclamations round the Cross.

This is strange when you think that the veneration which the Catholic Church gives to Mary is something that distinguishes it from other religions.

Every May Catholic churches with any sense of community spirit have a special Sunday afternoon ceremony to crown a statue of Mary with a chaplet of May flowers. The church is overrun with tiny children dressed in cotton and lace frocks, there's a procession of little girls like some pre-pubescent beauty contest, and everyone sings, 'Oh Mary we crown thee with blossoms today/Queen of the Angels and Queen of the May'. It's so sweet it almost makes you sick. And it incidentally confirms what you've long suspected: the Mother of God was a wimp.

She was herself conceived without sin (a mistake non-Catholics often make is to think the phrase 'immaculate conception' means she conceived Christ without having sex; she did that too, thanks to the Holy Ghost, but was herself the only human being born without original sin) and (implicitly) was unable to commit one all her life. There wasn't even any point in the Devil offering to tempt her. She instantly accedes to the wishes of the Lord when told by the Archangel Gabriel that the fruit of her womb would be Christ (I suppose it was a little late to try and complain); she and her astoundingly ineffectual husband Joseph are forced to flee from Israel by the depredations of King Herod; and when they return and set up the family home, she is treated with withering scorn by her delinquent Messiah. He backchats her when she complains about His habit of running away to discourse with the temple elders ('Woman, didst thou not know I must be about my father's business?'), and rarely shows her the least sign of affection or filial duty. When from the Cross He passes her on to St John ('Woman, behold thy Son; Son, behold thy mother') you feel as if she's been treated as an *adoptive parent* all his life.

There's something about the sweetly innocent, blue-eyed Virgin that stops her becoming a rôle-model to whole generations of convent schoolgirls: her passivity, her lack of spirit, her meekness in the face of dreadful privations. And it's possible to feel that the Church (for all its May crowning pap) doesn't care much for her either. She was never important, never taken seriously, never listened to, by God on earth. Will He listen to her supplications as she whispers to Him at the divine board-table?

SAINTS

The saints aren't part of the hierarchy, for some reason. They're like knights who've retired to Gloucestershire to take no further part in public life. For what they did so spectacularly on earth they have been rewarded with the classiest of designations, are prayed to constantly by their earthly fans, and can be found interceding directly on their behalf. They must therefore hold a high place in Heaven. Perhaps they sit in on board meetings, like British ex-MPs who turn up later as non-executive directors.

The most significant saints in the Catholic Emergency Phone Book are:

St Anthony, patron saint of lost things: his name is invoked fifty times a day by members of the faithful who have mislaid their reading glasses.

St Jude, patron of lost causes: invoked to cure seemingly endless attacks of dyspepsia, hiccups, sneezing and acne.

St Thérèse of Lisieux, a.k.a. the Little Flower: her reputation for childlike innocence concealed a tough-minded, indomitable nun. Usefully invoked by young women to grant either the grace of holy purity or the strength to tell some pestering jock where to get off.

St Joseph, husband to the Virgin Mary: often invoked as the paragon of patience, with good reason.

St Apollonia, patron of dentists: she had all her teeth knocked out, prior to being martyred. Her function is perhaps obvious.

St Thomas More: the gentle right-hand man of Henry VIII, martyred for opposing the royal divorce. Invoked by those who know they are right and hope the world will one day agree. Perhaps coincidentally, he is the patron saint of lawyers.

Meanwhile, back on earth, the hierarchy continues among the Lord's chosen representatives.

THE POPE

Medieval popes were a shockingly corrupt bunch. Some had wives, many had mistresses, several made un-Churchmanlike deals with warring kings. Throughout it all, the concept of Papal infallibility wobbled uncertainly along without ever being entirely discredited. Today, the Pope is still the chief voice of God on earth, whose word (theoretically) dictates the behaviour patterns of 500 million Catholics.

In my lifetime, there have been five: Pope Pius XII, Pope John XXIII, Pope Paul VI, Pope John Paul I and the current incumbent Pope John Paul II. Pius impinged on my senses only as an icon. His picture was featured on a garishly inscribed Papal Blessing tacked to the wall over my parents' bed. I regarded those stern features with a certain awe; how one ever got to sleep immediately beneath them (let alone anything else) was beyond me.

John XXIII, on the other hand, was the Pope of the century: a fat, smiling and wholly trustworthy Italian, he was credited with most of the major libertarian changes in the modern Catholic Church: the end of the Latin Mass; the turning round of the altar at Mass so that the priest now faced the congregation; the end of fasting and Friday abstinence; most of all, the relaxing of the strict rules that mostly confined nuns away from the outside world. His phrase about 'throwing open the windows' of closed orders reverberated through the Catholic world from Dublin to Warsaw.

Paul VI, following an unusually hard act, was a wizened and unfriendly-looking prelate, generally seen in public being carried shoulder-high in a mahogany throne. He took a harder line: his most famous move was the *Humanae Vitae* ruling in 1968 which effectively told the Catholics of the pill generation that they couldn't get away with it – that artificial contraception was still a no-no as far as the Church was concerned. The chief effect of this (as David Lodge has eloquently pointed out) was that for a time, a millimetre of rubber skin was all that lay between thousands of Catholics who did not want large families, and their faith.

John Paul I was a curiosity. He died within months of his accession to the Supreme Pontiff's throne, and was disingenuously hailed by the Catholic press as having had a purely symbolic rôle to play by virtue of his artlessly triumphant smile.

A sensationalist book by an investigative journalist made out that he'd been assassinated by vested interests in an alleged Catholic Mafia. It seemed unlikely: the only thing for which he was otherwise known was for writing *Illustrissimi*, a series of naïve inspirational letters to the likes of Pinocchio, urging chastity and obedience.

John Paul II, the present Pontiff, was a revelation for many reasons. He is a Pole, a poet and playwright, a skier, an indefatigable traveller, an ad-libber, a showman (all that kissing the tarmac at international airports), a glad-handing diplomat . . . and a thoroughgoing totalitarian. It's as if he is determined to test to destruction the idea of Papal infallibility, by issuing baffling and whimsical ex cathedra pronouncements: that there is no sex in Heaven (did anyone suggest there was?); that a man may commit adultery with his own wife if he regards her in the wrong way (i.e. as a sex object); that there can never be women priests because Christ's human essence was male (but then so was his being a Nazarene and a carpenter . . .).

The Pope is the head of the entire Church. He is also known as the Supreme Pontiff, the Vicar of Christ, the Bishop of Rome and the successor of St Peter – Christ's right-hand man among the Apostles in spite of his triple denial of his master in the Garden of Gethsemane. He therefore masterminds the spiritual direction of hundreds of millions of believers throughout the world. His word is law.

Stashed away in the Vatican is the secret rubric for choosing a Pope; hidden from secular eyes, it inevitably seems a little bizarre. Since the election of a man to the office of Pope is a democratic process among the cardinals – the uppermost wing of the Catholic hierarchy – it has the unique quality of being the fallible human selection of someone who will be God's infallible representative on earth. How can they tell? They sit in closed conference (nobody, it is said, can leave until they've picked a

winner) and vote by secret ballot. If the required majority of votes is not forthcoming, black smoke issues forth from the Vatican chimney-stack.

Then they all debate it further – how do the shortlisted names feel about being discussed so publicly? – and argue among themselves until finally deciding on the only true candidate. There can be no vote-rigging or string-pulling among the Church's holiest officers, so we must assume they are swayed by the word of God, as presented through the inspired arguments of the most vocal debaters. Once the appointment has been made, the grate is filled with whatever makes white smoke appear in the rooftop chimneys, the declaration of 'Habemus Papem' ('We have a Pope') is announced and the waiting crowd in St Peter's goes wild. The lucky new Pope goes to a robing room where three sizes of vestments (small, medium and large) await him. It is ironic that his first decision as head of the western world's largest Church is one more suited to the changing-rooms of Savile Row.

CARDINALS

Cardinals are the Catholic heads of countries, the uppermost authority to which to turn in any national dispute concerning religious matters. Their job is to 'advise and assist' the Pope in the government of the Church. It would be an unusually tough-minded cardinal, on the other hand, who tried to contradict the Pope or argue with his pronouncements. In Ireland the Cardinal is Tomas O'Fiach, who can sometimes be found denouncing the IRA; in England it's Basil Hume, an ex-monk of exceptionally kindly aspect who, you feel, would never be keen on denouncing anybody.

BISHOPS

Catholic bishops, ostensibly the descendants of Christ's other Apostles, are very grand Churchmen, often portly and clubbable like their Protestant counterparts, often clad in purple and sporting a huge ring for the faithful to kiss. They run a large, often city-wide manor called a diocese or see, lordly visit their parish priests every so often, and generally act like Japanese company chairmen. In the fifties and sixties, Catholic families with upwards of seven children could confidently expect a bishop to officiate at the Baptism of their next. It was like getting an Order of Lenin badge from the Politburo for spawning beyond the call of duty.

MONSIGNORS

These are usually parish priests who had come to the bishop's or cardinal's eye by their administrative efficiency. They are like senior civil servants, to be relied on for the smooth deliverance of an episcopal visit or a charity drive.

CANONS

Nobody knew how you got to be a canon, except through great age; it was assumed to be an honorary title, like one of those you get in Austria for being a retired businessman who never actually bankrupted any company; that and being able to radiate immense gravitas as you creakily descended the stairs from the choir gallery at the end of Sunday Mass. 'That's the canon,' the congregation would whisper to new members. 'Isn't he *marvellous?*'

THE MIDDLE-RANGE CLERGY

Catholics become priests and nuns for a variety of reasons, all of which have their provenance in childhood and adolescence. Every Catholic mother would like to have 'a son in Orders'; it represents the highest achievement of the strange secular vocation known as 'rearing children'.

In innumerable households the concept of the seminary or the convent raises its head at the point just after the first stirrings of intellectual ambitiousness and just before all the other stirrings. A difficult time for all concerned. Men become priests to please their mothers, to devote themselves to a higher good than accountancy or civil engineering, to avoid meeting girls or because they have been won over by the attractive exclusivity of the 'vocation'. In some famous cases, this has turned out to be a yen for showbusiness misinterpreted as a desire to show others the path to the supreme footlights.

In their search for new recruits, the powers that were always sought to persuade us that an apparent addiction to vice did not necessarily debar us from taking Holy Orders at some point. 'It's always the case,' untold nuns and priests have been heard to say, 'that it's always the naughtiest boy/girl in the school who becomes the priest/nun.' It was a prospect we hated, indeed dreaded. What if you had a vocation and didn't know it? It was like discovering you had a disease or finding that there was a bullet somewhere with your name on it. We hoped against hope we did *not* have one: unable to act either virtuous or disgracefully naughty (because both would attract the attention of the vocational press-gang) we chose a demure middle path and hoped to escape the accusing finger of God.

THE GOOD PRIEST GUIDE

The Academics: fiftyish to seventyish. Tended to embrace with relish a top-level ruling that sermons should help the congregation interpret some knotty point of linguistic or philosophical symbolism in the Sunday morning Epistle. Invariably led to twenty-five-minute dissertations on the views of Aquinas or Heidegger. Did little for the ranks of charladies and flower-sellers in the first ten rows. Ensured profound sleep for those left ungripped by phenomenology, eschatology or Hebraic phonemes.

The Irascibles: fortyish to fifty-fiveish. Tended to slap altar boys across the face for insolence. Sticklers for protocol at Mass, they would think nothing of haranguing a funeral procession for steering itself the wrong way. At their best carrying a monstrance with a look on their face that suggested they'd reached their deserved level of dignity. Became teachers and administered punishment, necks getting redder by the minute. Several undisclosed homosexuals among them, keen on arm wrestling. Obsessed by obedience, never (of course) to themselves but always to the greater glory of God. We knew what they meant though. We knew who was boss.

The Chummies: twenty-fiveish to forty. These were the local curates who befriended the youth of the district, started clubs whose treasurers ran off with the petty cash in the fourth week, initiated folk singing during Easter week and tried to dissuade a whole generation of pop stars manqués from infiltrating 'Let It Be' and 'Lady Madonna' into the ceremonials. They were the golf players and the treaters, who'd take you to the movies to see *2001: A Space Odyssey* and *Lawrence of Arabia* and question you on the way home about how they were regarded in the neighbourhood. They drove Hillman Avengers and Vauxhall Vivas which smelt of plimsolls. They would uncomprehendingly lend you a dog-collar for a tarts 'n' vicars party, and be unsure how to tell you off once they'd found out.

The Youngbloods: twentyish to thirty-five. Nervous, pink round the neck and wet behind the ears, they were straight out of college. Newly embarked on 'pastoral duties', they were just discovering to their horror that these involved visiting some very decrepit, desperate and above all ungrateful matrons in the south London back streets. Retreated with audible relief to the bourgeois living-rooms where they would be 'taken up' by professional-class wives and introduced to Rotarians who addressed them as 'Padre'. A taste for sixth-form debate lingered in their fireside chats with the children. Unfortunately, a lack of experience meant that their hard-line rigour, confronted by adolescent querulousness, led to exasperation. 'Look,' they'd say, with a conclusive snort, 'if you can't accept *that*, then you can't call yourself a Catholic at all.' Retreated to their frugal parish HQ, complete with nagging landlady, to lie awake fretting about their transcendent soul. Many left the priesthood shortly after, to become travel agents.

NUNS

Nuns were the strangest apparitions to make an impression on one's childhood. Eccentric uncles, muttering drunks in the street, church-going madmen, funfair clowns, seven-foot Goofys shaking your hand at the Easter parade in Battersea Park – they all, like Keith Waterhouse's Uncle Mad, make a mark on your early memories. But none retains that special intensity of effect on your psyche as the arrival of the nun in your life.

KAREN ARMSTRONG

Everyone there was amazed when I wanted to be a nun. But I always objected to the brides of Christ, all that white-veils stuff. I felt Mary was no rôle-model. That was left to Christ; God was an utterly perfect being who knew you through and through. I was very conscious of wanting to get rid of myself into a perfect being, to immerse myself in perfection.

However kindly, frail and sweet-faced they were, however young, teacherish and bossy they were, however cheery, raucous-voiced and gamesome they were, nuns always carried an air of trouble. They were the enemy, no doubt about it. They looked threatening, with their black, armour-plated uniforms and out-size black Rosaries, a sharp metallic crucifix dangling among the beads that rattled on their skirts as they strode by.

Before it was discontinued, the habit of the Sisters of Mercy used to feature a hat of crazed design: a stiff white cardboard zig-zag that flew out from either side of the head like spiky multiple wings, and made the smiling wearer look like some pterodactylic predator, about to eat you up. On my first encounter with this intriguing fashion item – meeting my nun auntie when I was three – I instantly flooded my new corduroy shorts and yelled for an hour.

The rest of the ensemble was clearly designed for maximum scare effect. The teaching- and nursing-order nuns of London in the sixties (whatever was the case with their closed-order counterparts) resembled a Samurai élite, a black-clad Moorish horde that El Cid would have thought twice about keeping in line. Check out that Sister Xavier Maria look:

- the face is tightly swaddled in stiff, shiny cardboard overlaid by some scratchy black crêpy material last seen gracing the dusty drawing-room curtains of Miss Havisham in David Lean's film of *Great Expectations*;
- the bosom, or any hint thereof, was firmly restrained beneath a chilly half-circle of white Formica that started at the neck and reached as far as the armpits. From a certain angle this concave bodice resembled the nastily rounded axe-blade in Vincent Price's *The Pit and the Pendulum*;
- the habit, on some of the more substantial-looking sisters, looked vastly enveloping, like the billowing top-gallant of a three-masted sloop. On the more angular nuns, it went straight up and down, like a bombazine-wrapped statue. It was always jet black, coarsely textured and conveyed a sense of impenetrability. No jute coal-sack seemed more impermeable. No medieval chain-mail chemise looked less likely to admit a marauding intruder. We never got close enough to stroke this fascinating garment (not an activity that would have been

encouraged) and so could not establish of what material (fustian? calico?) it was made. Perhaps it was as well to remain in ignorance;

• the scarcely optional accessories — economy-size Rosary around waist, industrial-strength crucifix on reinforced-steel hawser around neck, Adolf Eichmann spectacles, dark black court jackboots . . .

_____CLARE TOYNBEE_____

In the convent sixth form, when we would read Shakespeare, we noticed how the nuns always took the best rôles themselves. The sisters would invariably tell you that the naughtiest girls in the school were the ones that turned out to have a vocation. As a result I went around desperately trying to be good and hoping like mad that I didn't have any such thing.

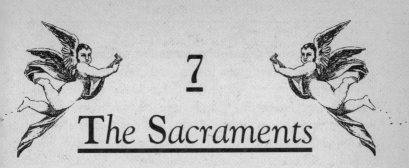

7
The Sacraments

What is a Sacrament?
A Sacrament is an outward sign of inward grace, ordained by Jesus Christ, by which grace is given to our souls.

Whence have the Sacraments the power of giving grace?
The Sacraments have the power of giving grace from the merits of Christ's Precious Blood, which they apply to our souls.

Ought we to have a great desire to receive the Sacraments?
We ought to have a great desire to receive the Sacraments, because they are the chief means of our Salvation.

THE SACRAMENTS ARE BIG OCCASIONS in the life of the average Catholic. They're the most serious manifestations of one's Catholicity, and (by a kind of quid pro quo) one's acknowledgment of the importance of the Church at the key moments of one's career. They are the times when the faithful are allowed to approach a new and closer relationship with God, by entering into one of seven states: Baptism, Confirmation, Penance, Holy Eucharist, Matrimony, Holy Orders and the Anointing of the Sick.

Each time you take part in a sacramental ritual, you're told, you become filled with 'sanctifying grace', which will wash your mucky soul to purest white (provided you're worthy of such transcendent laundering), and leave you mentally renewed, spiritually pristine and ready to fight, as though joining the army of God again for the first time, the omnipresent cohorts of Satan.

Some sacraments can be received only once (Baptism, Confirmation, Ordination); some are expected to become a habit with the believer (Confession and Communion). The Final Anointing (also known as Extreme Unction, also known as the Last Rites) are supposedly reserved for one's deathbed; but there is nothing to stop the indestructible and the hypochondriacal receiving it again and again, provided a priest judges it suitable. The last of the seven, Marriage, is also technically supposed to be a one-off, but due to the complicated legal niceties concerning annulment and the like in the Catholic rule book, the Supreme Being can theoretically be encouraged to smile on one's union with several people.

There is another way of expressing this. Receiving the three one-off sacraments constitutes the Church's official stamp of approval; it means that you're accepted among the faithful, taken on board, tested and passed, and – should you have taken the enormous step into Holy Orders – finally received among the hierarchy. In societal terms, they meant you had matriculated, graduated and were ultimately allowed into Who's Who.

Engaging with the rituals of Confession and Communion, by contrast, was more like garaging the Ford Sierra of your soul for a weekly servicing, complete with oil change, re-fuel, a top-up of air and a thorough wash 'n' waxing. Confession and Communion were injections of the pleasing concept of sanctifying grace into recalcitrant and accident-prone machinery. The qualifying notion that their recipient would only derive the full benefit if he or she was properly prepared – devout, humble, contrite about one's shortcomings – was often lost amid the mundane forces of habit that drew you to confessional box and altar rails.

BAPTISM

Perhaps the most problematic of the sacraments, Baptism tends to happen without your knowledge or consent. Hard-line Catholic mothers are notorious, when confronted by lapsing teenage offspring, for demanding to know how they can 'turn their back' on a heritage to which they were forcibly and unilaterally introduced at the font.

Catholic Baptism follows much the same pattern as the Protestant christening service. Few godparents seriously expect that they'll be called out of the blue one day to take charge of some infant's 'spiritual direction'. They are there as the parents' chums and the children's allies and rôle-models; they are chosen because their naturally kindly disposition, their flash contacts, their money or career status will at some point guarantee an easier life for their charges.

Catholic godparents are expected to take things more seriously. As well as renouncing Satan (a piece of cake, usually), they must promise to keep the hapless infant on the highway of the one true faith. Not the vague, Christian path of humanistic virtue, but the main Catholic M-road to Heaven. There's a small but distinct whiff of the press-gang about the operation.

CONFIRMATION

It's generally assumed that when you reach the Augustanly-entitled 'age of reason' (at about seven years) your childish thought-processes will have a sufficient grasp of Catholic theology – over and above the set of beliefs instilled in you from infancy – to decide for yourself what you make of the Church. You will therefore be in a position to make a tacit choice to abide by the Church's teaching and laws.

There is, of course, no choice involved. No parent or teacher is going to sidle up to you one day and ask, 'Look, are you sure you wouldn't rather be a Zen Buddhist?' or, 'Marie-Rose, can you really accept Pannenberg's refutations of the doctrine of transubstantiation and still call yourself a Catholic?' Rather, you're congratulated on having grown up enough to be a feeling, thinking part of the Great Family.

You and your little peer group sit together in a crowded church one evening, away from your families, feeling frightfully serious about your new status, before approaching the altar rails in a shuffling crocodile, there to be addressed in a fruity mutter by a visiting bishop who concludes your brief colloquy with a light cuff around the head – ostensibly to remind you that being, and remaining, a Catholic won't be all beer and skittles. You can choose a new name to be added to those attached to you at Baptism. It can't, regrettably, be any trendy handle you've come to admire – Duke, Marlon, Clint, Rock – more a respectful tip of the hat at a respectable saint, like Francis (as in St Francis Xavier) or Ignatius (of Loyola), the strategic Jesuit choices.

CATHOLIC NAMES

Tradition plays a considerable part in the naming of young Catholics. It's not that families check through the lives of the saints in search of something suitable; it's simply that the names have been in the families for several generations – or, if not sanctioned by time, had at least turned up in the outlying reaches of second and third cousins in extremely large Papist families over a mere generation or two.

Traditional names (girls): Marie, Mary, Mary-Louise, Mary-Bernadette, Mary-Geraldine, Magdalene (very tricky this one; only found in the acceptably French variant of Madeleine), Elizabeth, Margaret/Peggy, Anne, Anne-Marie/Bernadette/Geraldine, Theresa, Bernadette, Bridie/Bridget, Cecilia, Carmel/Carmelita, Angela, Concepta (meaning 'Conceived' but with the implication of 'Without Sin'), Imelda (despite the down-market associations of Mrs Marcos)

Traditional names (boys): John (the Beloved/the Baptist), Paul, Peter, Andrew, Anthony, Thomas (despite his doubts), Michael, Patrick (very suitable – an Englishman who converted Ireland . . .), Martin, Francis Xavier (the most tell-tale initials in the Catholic gazetteer), Ignatius, James, Dennis

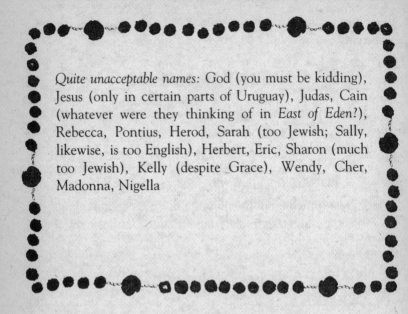

Quite unacceptable names: God (you must be kidding), Jesus (only in certain parts of Uruguay), Judas, Cain (whatever were they thinking of in *East of Eden?*), Rebecca, Pontius, Herod, Sarah (too Jewish; Sally, likewise, is too English), Herbert, Eric, Sharon (much too Jewish), Kelly (despite Grace), Wendy, Cher, Madonna, Nigella

CONFESSION

Confession is the key sacrament, in some ways the most potent of them all in conveying at least the illusion that you're forgiven everything you've done wrong, washed to a newly virtuous shine, and let out into the sunlight to start all over again, only this time being good. It brought a wonderful sense of release. It made you feel spiritually invigorated, grateful and unusually anxious to please. For the few moments that post-Confession euphoria lasted before you got home and started acting like Vlad the Impaler all over again, it made you believe in redemption.

What you most vividly remember, however, is sliding reluctantly along a wax-polished pew in the wake of a couple of dozen evil-smelling parishioners, in the dark corner of an almost silent and fusty church at three thirty on a Saturday afternoon, worrying over the final details of your speech.

—————————— FRANK O'CONNOR ——————————

. . . It was my turn now. With the fear of damnation in my soul I went in, and the confessional door closed of itself behind me.

It was pitch dark and I couldn't see the priest or anything else. Then I really began to be frightened. In the darkness it was a matter between God and me, and he had all the odds. He knew what my intentions were before I even started; I had no chance. All I had ever been told about Confession got mixed up in my mind, and I knelt to one wall and said: 'Bless me, Father, for I have sinned; this is my first confession.' I waited for a few minutes but nothing happened, so I tried it on the other wall. Nothing happened there either. He had me spotted all right.

Examining your conscience was the first step, they said. Ask your innermost self what it felt most ashamed of, teach it to range over the last few weeks' activities like some sternly moral metal detector, until some internal bleeping noise could be heard coming from the soul and you knew you'd hit on something.

That was the theory. In practice, you tended to use a formula, a decoy list of unexceptionable transgressions, the small change of the Confession world. On to this, if you were feeling genuinely contrite (unlikely) or genuinely worried (far more likely), you could graft sins of more serious import, and fervently hope they wouldn't be noticed.

'Bless me, Father, for I have sinned. It is three weeks since my last Confession and these are my sins: I, er, was disobedient to my parents on three occasions. I took the name of God in vain on three occasions. I was late for Mass on one occasion (keep going, keep going). I, er, struck someone in anger twice. And (here it comes – just slip it in at the last moment) I, errrrm (spit it out) entertempurthawnoccasion . . .'

'Come again?' the still figure on the other side of the grille would enquire, with the air of a man who has all the time in the world.

Deep breath. 'Bless me, Father . . .'

'Not the whole lot, boy. Just that last bit you rushed through.'

Oh no. Oh bloody hell. 'I said I, errrrm (please, earth, open up and swallow me) I have entertained impure thoughts on several occasions.'

'I see.' He leans sideways. 'Were you alone or with others?'

What can he mean? Does he imagine that I can't think unless there are other people around? 'I was alone.'

'And how far did you entertain them?'

(Surely it should be 'How far did they entertain you?' Then you could give them a rating, as though choosing your Films of the Year.)

You are beginning to hate this line of enquiry. 'I thought about them quite a lot.' ('They' were the spectacular breasts of Miss Ursula Andress in *Doctor No.*)

'Did you commit a further sin when thinking in this way?'

Eeurgh. Don't be so disgusting. 'I don't know what you—'

'Did you indulge in the sin of self-abuse?'

'No, Father.' Then, 'Certainly not', in that prissy, what-kind-of-girl-do-you-take-me-for voice. Before you're fully apprised about masturbation and how, if it doesn't necessarily lead to blindness, it makes a terrible mess of the soul, the expression 'self-abuse' would fall on the ear like a synonym for suicide. Really, it's far too intense a subject to discuss in the dark with a total stranger through a section of wire mesh.

'Temptations are everywhere, my son. Wicked books and

plays and pictures and films. These mini-skirts. This immorality and permissiveness . . .'

'Mmmmmmmm.' My head was nodding up and down in silent endorsement of all the things on his list that made life worth living.

'. . . It makes it all worth while, when you've made the effort to resist these temptations, to feel you've said to the Devil, "Get thee behind me, Satan," and succeeded. So give up the dirty films, my son, and learn to think of women with a proper respect, and to think of the human body as a vessel of the Holy Ghost, which must not be contaminated . . .'

On and on he would drone, offering gratuitous advice on impossible matters; it just wasn't physically possible to resist going to see *From Russia With Love*, precisely to get a fix of heroically vicarious smut. But you were safe now that you'd got to this lecture stage. There'd be no further grilling about just

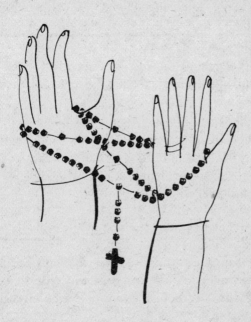

what you got up to, no delicate circumlocutions about 'Petting' and 'Intimacy'. All you were sticking around for was to intone the Act of Contrition ('Oh, my God, I am heartily sorry for having offended Thee...') and learn what was your punishment.

One's penance rarely altered from the standard rate of one Our Father and three Hail Marys, unless you'd thrown in something deliberately controversial (suicide attempt, conversion to Communism, armed robbery). Sentence was always dished out in the form of prayers – it was hardly a real punishment, more like spending a few weeks on community service.

────────────────CLARE TOYNBEE────────────────

Once my mother was left inside a confessional by mistake for forty-five minutes by a priest who didn't realise she was still there and went off to his tea-break. God only knows what the people in the church made of it when she finally emerged.

Part of the vast sense of relief that swept over the departing ex-sinner was the way in which the most terrifying, unimaginable, light-years-long punishment that hung over you when you entered the confessional was mysteriously commuted (for good behaviour?) to a few muttered prayers on your way out. It didn't make sense – but one was hardly disposed to quibble about such a pleasingly low-key penal code . . .

────────────────HARRY ARMFIELD────────────────

The biggest dilemma you faced was that you couldn't go to Communion unless you'd first gone to Confession. If you'd committed a sin of 'thought, word or deed' you had to go to

Confession. But what if, between the two sacraments you managed to commit *another* sin?

I remember the Easter when I was thirteen. I'd been to Confession on Easter Saturday morning, and, because of the celebrations the next day, had to go for a haircut in the afternoon. At the barber's there was a whole pile of girlie magazines, from *Titbits* to *Fiesta*, which I couldn't resist. By the time I got to the barber's chair, I'd whizzed through them all, and by now was saturated with impure thoughts for someone called Amber Smith.

The next day I was in a quandary. You can't very well *not* go to Communion on Easter Sunday, because your parents will wonder what you've been getting up to and grill you later. But if you did go, you'd be committing a mortal sin because you'd received a sacrament while in a state of sin . . .

Who do you please, God or your parents? I was still thinking about Ms Amber Smith as I went up the aisle, before my family and the whole congregation, to receive the sacred body of Jesus, in the certain knowledge that I'd committed a worse sin than murder . . .

COMMUNION

It's supposed to be the most glorious moment, when you receive the Body of Christ in the form of a Host placed upon your tongue, and have it dissolve inside you. It's meant to be the most perfect consummation between a perfect, all-loving God and the horribly flawed sinners of the average congregation. Why then does the simple act of going up to Communion inspire such nervousness, such paranoia, such a tirade of inappropriate reactions?

━━━━━━━━━━━━ANTHONY BURGESS━━━━━━━━━━

I was seven now, and hence had arrived at the age of reason. I had to become a rational son of the Church by making my first confession and by taking my first communion . . . The morning of my first communion should have been the happiest moment of my life. It was, up to that point, the most terrifying. I was given the Body and Blood of Jesus Christ in the form of a thin wafer that cleaved to the roof of my mouth, and I came away from the altar, hands joined, eyes closed, murmuring, 'My Lord and My God'. I could clear Christ away from my palate with my tongue, but hellfire awaited if my teeth touched him. If even a morsel of food or a droplet of liquid had preceded his ingestion, then heaven would rage and fresh coal be trundled in against my sudden and unrepentant death. It became, from the moment of being a full communicant, very important to put off death. I made my first communion with Manchester rain beating down. On my way to Church I had opened my mouth to receive a few drops. Was that liquid nourishment? From now on, I had to be good. I had qualified for Hell.

(From *Little Wilson and Big God*, Penguin, 1988)

It's guilt, that's why. It's because the joyous consummation you've been told so much about requires you to be 1 good; 2 truthful about your recent transgressions; 3 wholeheartedly sorry for your sins; and 4 thinking of nothing but your Saviour. Most of the time, you're none of the four. Hence the huge numbers who, brazenly still in a state of sin, proceed up the aisle to that hushed, ineffable moment of communication, and find themselves returning to it years later, whimpering with guilt and howling to be saved.

Sometimes it was the unconfessed sins from the previous day's confessions. Sometimes you would be nagged at by the memory of something you'd done the night before. Sometimes it would be because you had failed to comply with the rules of fasting when the fasting laws were still operational. Originally, you weren't allowed to eat anything from midnight until the moment of Communion (a bit tough on the six thirty p.m. Mass-goers). This was changed to a three-hour embargo on food, which soon shrank to a one-hour; but since Communion mostly falls forty minutes into a fifty-minute Mass, this was a pointless rule except for those actually scoffing bacon sandwiches on their way into church.

The Host is a small circlet of wafery bread, upon which (as far as one's peripheral vision can tell) an image of the crucified Christ is embossed. A whole loaf-equivalent of Hosts are kept in beautifully ornate silver chalices in the altar tabernacle, awaiting the moment when the priest announces their transformation into the divine Body and Blood.

REBECCA FRASER

Before I took my first Holy Communion, I was given religious instruction in a different church which made me feel rather superior. But the day itself was terrifying; I had to fast three hours before the ceremony, after which I would have lunch with my godparents. I wore a long white dress and a veil and, almost absentmindedly, I ate a little segment of crystallised orange. I thought something dreadful was about to happen to me.

Were one to examine them in their secular, untransformed state, they would probably seem far from prepossessing. But when infused with all the significance of Heaven and Eternity, the Hosts had an extraordinary power. They were like nothing else you ever had in your mouth. They tended to cling immovably to the palate roof, until they disintegrated, leaving a faint, not unpleasant taste like the smell of musty parchment. It didn't seem like food – more like some medicine, professionally administered by a tall grown-up, who instructed you (tacitly of course) not to muck about with it, because it was good for you.

You were not, under any circumstances, to touch the Host with your teeth – as if one were trying to consume one's Maker, like the Wolf munching up Little Red Riding Hood's Granny – nor actually to touch the thing with your finger. And as for going any further . . . A story was circulated to successive generations of schoolboys, presumably to discourage the more enquiring minds, about a naughty boy who told his mates that today at Mass he was going to find out exactly what was written or stamped on the Host. He'd take it out of his mouth after Communion, hide it and show them afterwards. Well, he duly *did* remove the transubstantiated Body of Our Redeemer, and (disgrace beyond belief) secreted it in his handkerchief. After Mass (the teacher's voice would tremble a bit here) his little friends gathered round as he unfolded the handkerchief, to reveal, not the much-abused Host, but instead a *drop of blood* . . . !

8
The Catholic
Hardware Department

EVERY CATHOLIC retains from childhood a secret drawer in an otherwise wholly secular desk, in which lurk the paraphernalia of belief. It may be a tacky string necklace with a dangling rectangle of waxy paper on which the image of the Blessed Virgin is faintly inscribed. It may be a familiar roundel of ivory or glass beads leading to a miniaturised crucifix. It may be a medal, an inspirational card, a once-treasured Mass book, but it'll be there somewhere. Childhood devotion to these objects may dwindle, but the time somehow never comes when you can simply hurl them into a dustbin of life's outgoings.

Although the Catholic Church is far from keen on graven images and lucky amulets kept for reasons of superstition (the first Commandment expressly forbids 'trusting to charms, omens, dreams and such-like fooleries'), its adherents positively dote on them. But the Church has only itself to blame: for no other religion (although Judaism comes close) throws up such a variety of quasi-religious knick-knacks whose purpose is to remind the individual of the Root of his Being and the Object of his Devotion.

STATUES

The Buddhists probably have more statues per capita than the Catholic fraternity, but they're statues of the Great Man and nobody else. Although Buddha was a teacher rather than a god, many Buddhists regard him as having a direct effect upon their lives, and bring offerings of incense and flowers to sweeten their requests that their families will be successful, healthy and long-lived.

Catholic churches are more profligate about their statuary. While Christ Himself is more usually portrayed dying on the Cross, His mother, His lieutenants the Apostles, His disciples, His prophets and random saints, are all granted a share of the action. All are instantly recognisable, due to a kind of divine typecasting, an iconographic shorthand.

St Francis of Assisi is invariably given a sparrow on the tips of his right hand. St Martin de Porres (the Church's token black saint) is always in white to highlight his skin colour. St Patrick's feet are a-writhe with departing heathen snakes. The Virgin Mary is always a vision in blue and white, for ever caught in her mid-twenties looking sad but understanding (although at that age she would hardly have been married, let alone seen her only son being crucified). St Vincent de Paul is a bearded roughneck in seafarer's rags. St Joseph is invariably given the rôle of acquiescent dotard, with a bald head and walking-frame staff to emphasise his decrepitude.

You were perfectly entitled to deposit flowers or light candles around the feet of whichever saint especially took your fancy as long as it was clearly understood that you weren't actually thinking of worshipping them. That would be a shocking liturgical *canard*. The only object of worship was God (or Christ, which is of course the same thing); anybody else was a downstream operator, a middle-ranks apparatchik, a League Division Two impostor. You could like or admire them, ask them to intercede with the Lord and pull a few strings for you, but that was it. And you never, under any circumstances, were caught mistakenly worshipping a lump of china or porcelain for its own sake.

PICTURES

The most famous Catholic picture of all is, unsurprisingly, of God. More specifically, it's of the Sacred Heart, one of the more gory incarnations of the Godhead, brought to a million calm suburban walls with a literal-mindedness that beggars belief. It shows the long-haired, beautiful but unsmiling figure of Christ extending a long hand towards you and indicating with the other his exposed, ruined heart. Its shape and colour are a typical cardiac strawberry, and from it beams of light are streaming like the Pearl and Dean advertisement in the cinema.

What its significance could have been was a mystery and remains one to this day. Did it mean Christ gave his heart for our sins? (Hardly.) That he loves us? (Too sentimental – it wouldn't account for the flayed aorta.) That Christ's emotional side should engage us just as much as his teaching and his rational debate? (Perhaps the most plausible – but it's surely a slightly gross way of displaying one's credentials as a sentient being.)

What increased our childish bafflement about this image was the reverence with which it was treated: you'd think it was a shrine, not just a picture. A small red-tinted lightbulb would be wired up to burn before it day and night, like some bad-taste commercial for open-heart surgery. Every Catholic home seemed to have one, glowing with feeble menace in hallway and landing.

MEDALS

Everyone was given medals on special days: First Communion medals, Confirmation medals, medals of obscure saints, intercessionary medals, prayer-supplement medals; but most ubiquitous was the 'miraculous medal', a nondescript oval of thin tin alloy, which one safety-pinned to one's jacket, trousers, pyjamas, and other essential bits of clothing. Girls would keep them in the medal section of their Catholic handbags. A birthday-present wallet would inevitably be found to feature a medal pinned in the soft material near the zip.

Their generic name (Miraculous Medals!) had, you will agree, a decided resonance; and indeed many people believed that the bits of metal were indeed instinct with the power to perform astounding paranormal feats, rather than merely commemorate the 'miraculous' nature of Christ. The way they were pressed on you at exam-time, or when you went rock-climbing in the Cairngorms during the holidays, underlined their apparent value as a shield against bad luck.

The least endearing medal commemorated the Little Infant Jesus of Prague on an elaborately wrought red background. Why the Czech version of a juvenile Christ should find any favour with the English or Irish – who generally prefer to see him as a hippie, a demagogue, or a willowy Prince Hamlet – has never been established. But the medals were everywhere, urged upon us by fat Catholic aunties as though representing some kind of rôle-model. They displayed the Son of God as a kind of Little Lord Fauntleroy, a sickly-looking doll in a sateen frock, awkwardly holding up a parliamentary mace like a magic wand.

My father claimed to have parked a Little Infant medal under his answer papers when sitting his final exams at medical school. His handwriting apparently unaffected by this bizarre stratagem, he passed them all with flying colours, and put an unshakeable trust in the efficacy of the Czech Messiah for the rest of his life. To any queries as to whether his religious belief was being compromised by mere superstition, he would loftily reply: 'I've told you a hundred times – keep the faith, or you'll never have a day's luck . . .'

ROSARIES

From the colossal beaded lassos that the Ursuline nuns dangled from their belted habits, to the discreet little prayer wheels (ten spokes and a tiny crucifix) that were slowly twirled round the finger by embarrassed praying types on the Tube, the Rosary epitomised the public Catholic devotee and the private Catholic family unit. Its essential function was as a numerical aid to prayer: the ten beads in a 'decade' told off the ten Hail Marys, the single bead between decades signified both the initial Our Father or the closing Glory Be. Each of the five decades on a typical Rosary enunciated a part of the New Testament – an occasion, an event – and the commemorative quintets were given the ringing titles of 'The Joyful Mysteries', 'The Sorrowful Mysteries' and 'The Glorious Mysteries'.

The first dealt with the arrival on earth of Jesus Christ – the Announcement to the Virgin Mary of her imminent pregnancy, the Nativity, etc.; the second, the Sorrowful ones, were all about the Passion and death (the Agony in the Garden, the Scourging, the Crucifixion); and the final five concerned the rapture of his Resurrection and Ascension into Heaven. Only some of them were authentic 'mysteries', meaning unexplained phenomena (like the impregnation of the Virgin, her own Immaculate status, her Assumption into Heaven and so on). The others were more familiar highlights from the more exciting bits of the

Gospels. But they were included specifically so that you could reflect on each of them, gravely and humbly, while praying to the Lord.

Saying the same prayer (Hail Mary full of grace, the Lord is with thee etc.) ten times consecutively for each 'mystery' had a curiously satisfying effect: its high boredom quotient, its relentless, question-and-answer chant, induced a state of mild hypnosis. You could feel your eyes beginning to stare, your jaw to droop, your whole upper frame to sway. Involuntarily entranced as you mouthed the responses ('HOLY Mary Mother of God, prayfruss sinners now 'nthehour of our deathayMEN'), your thoughts took off into free-associating flight.

I used to indulge in elaborate macho fantasies, partly based on *The Man From Uncle*, partly on *Rawhide* and partly on the Gospels: there I was springing an exhausted but grateful Christ ('getting a bit hairy out there . . . Knew you'd come . . . thanks,

old boy') from the Garden of Gethsemane; here I am talking back to Pontius Pilate, his cheeks suffused with impotent rage ('Caramba!' he would hiss, like the Mediterranean villains in the *New Hotspur*. 'Thees Eengleesh dog has outweetted me!'); check out how I let my eyes flicker amusedly at the chap who (what is he, *kidding?*) had the nerve to stick a crown of thorns on my forehead and strike me with a palm frond, before I let him have it with the customised Buntline Special secreted in my sock.

A young woman of my acquaintance confessed that in her teens she spent the twenty-minute span of the daily Family Rosary carving a couple more names for her projected brood of children (all boys) on to the underseats of the wooden kitchen chairs. 'Philip' the chairs announced to anyone who came into unusually close contact with them, 'Jason, Richard, Alexander, Sebastian, Xerxes . . .' Even the names of sundry household pets were added as her maternal inspiration dwindled.

Other people remembering these familial drone-ins chose to meditate on sexual matters, or wondered how they could afford the prices at the Chelsea Drugstore the following Saturday, or itemised the number of Party Seven cans they'd need for a proper birthday do, or just wished to God (the nearest they got to prayer) the exams didn't loom over everything like a thunder-cloud. It was not the most successful exercise in devotional solidarity.

RELICS

Relics occupied the disgusting-but-fascinating end of the hard-ware section. They were often to be found in the crucifixes of old Rosaries. When you'd unscrewed a little screw and lifted up the back of the crucifix (it swung on a hinge), there on a muslin ribbon lay the relic in splendour.

Sometimes it was a 'fragment of the True Cross'. Or was it? Some impious body once calculated that the combined weight of alleged fragments of the True Cross around the world and down the centuries would equal upwards of a thousand Scandinavian pine forests. What we actually held in our hands was both impressive (in mystery) and disappointing (in ordinariness). The tiny lump of *lignum vitae* or burnt mahogany that stood in for the cedar of Calvary might well (for all we knew) possess the appropriate antiquity – but did it radiate holiness and truth? Not really. Perhaps we expected too much from slivers.

More rare was the fragment of a saint's clothing you could occasionally buy in a Catholic Repository (i.e. shop) on the Continent, especially in the rougher bits of southern Italy. It would either be sewn on to a framed representation of the Cross, or be found inside a Rosary, or have a whole picture-frame to itself. 'It' was no more that a one-square-millimetre dot of fabric, lightly encrusted with mould or dust or some dark liquid. (Jamaican rum? Blood?) Generally it was accompanied by an explanatory paragraph, saying it was from the tunic of St Gerald Majella, the wimple of St Teresa of Avila or the waterproof headband of St Vincent. Its look of crumbly decay made you loth to enquire further.

The same, in spades, goes for the final class of relic. These were bits of the actual bodies of holy people – a mild indulgence in the frisson of necrophilia, in the interests of encouraging the modern owner to greater religious zeal. All you saw was a tiny smear of what might have been skin, or possibly some insect long shrivelled by the Neapolitan sun. No reassuring document ever told you the exact provenance of these unlovely bits of tissue. Which portion of which saint's anatomy I carried proudly in my school satchel all those months I shall, thankfully, never know.

The largest, most dramatic and most unsettling relic I ever found was in a handsome Catholic church in Drogheda, a small town on Ireland's north-east coast. On the altar steps (causing Lord knows what traumas to succeeding generations of servers), in a lantern-like glass case set in a gilt frame, you used to be able to gaze upon the actual head of Blessed (now Saint) Oliver Plunkett. Sentenced by Cromwell to be hanged, drawn and quartered and his body thrown to ravening hounds, he was rescued – a little late perhaps – before the dogs could get at him, and his head transferred in glory to the church steps. Is it how he would like to be remembered? Do many people, inspired by his example, pray for the grace to meet the same end? I wonder.

SCAPULARS

Technically the word means 'of the shoulderblade', a piquantly worldly definition of a defiantly spiritual accoutrement. A scapular is a strange green object, a string necklace like a US army dogtag. It ends in a papery lozenge that bears the figure of the Blessed Virgin dressed in a shawl and surrounded by clouds, holding twin hearts before her bosom. Uniquely among Catholic ornaments, it is not meant to be seen at all, but to be worn beneath the shirt or blouse as a constant, itchy reminder of the Divine Presence.

You don't see many of them on sale nowadays; even twenty years ago they were offered to the young faithful with a certain distaste. This is presumably because they were the last, unlamented relics of the mildly barbaric hair-shirt tradition, which encouraged believers to mortify the flesh by voluntarily inflicting themselves with pain.

The tradition – and its extreme forms of fleshly mortification, such as the self-flagellation of young would-be monks in enclosed orders – reached its apogee in the person of a Dublin down-and-out called Matt Talbot, who one day saw a blinding revelation of

Divine suffering and reformed his life. He gave up drink, turned to prayer and good works, and wound painful, sharp-edged chains around his body to emulate the suffering of Christ. When he died and the evidence of his devotion was discovered (hushed Irish voices will tell you) the links had to be cut away from his bloodied flesh. Today there's a bridge in Dublin named after him. After England's Elizabethan monopoly of the breed, Dublin is proud to have a martyr of its very own.

9

The Catholic Community

A *RICH AND VARIED SELECTION* of metaphors exists by which to describe the generality of Catholics known as the Church. From the Gospels we inherited the mildly patronising notion that we were unusually dim sheep in need of constant guidance and protection. In the hymns of childhood, we appear as a beleaguered army, an ark of believers or a storm-battered citadel – the iconography of, for example, 'Star of the Sea':

> Deep night hath come down on this rough-spoken world,
> And the banners of darkness are boldly unfurled.
> And the tempest-tossed Church, all her eyes are on Thee,
> They look to Thy shining bright Star of the Sea.

Elsewhere, according to the likes of the late Cardinal Heenan, the Church is to be regarded by new adherents as a comfy-cosy giant family, to whom new members gravitate for reasons of love, and within which all is harmonious fellow-feeling and mutual regard. Whether you favour the benign or the militaristic reading – or lean towards some alternative view, say of the Church as some vast secular banking conglomerate – the

Catholic community is perhaps most usefully seen as the sum total of all the congregations you have ever known.

There's the glum, scanty and unhealthy-complexioned devotees of a Battersea church where I attended Mass every Sunday. There was the far more glamorous Redemptorist congre-

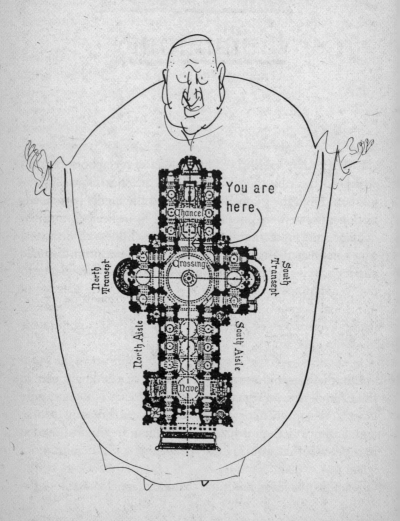

gation at St Mary's Clapham, where the avuncular priests essayed little jokes from the pulpit and asked for money with laughing roguishness. There were the subtly, but ineffably grand convocations of minor Kensingtonian gentry (tracing their Romish lineage back before the Reformation) at Brompton Oratory and Westminster Cathedral; and the passionately devout, seat-cramming multitudes that packed the churches of western Ireland where I went for my teenage vacations. A disparate and various bunch; but each gathering, in its different way, affirmed something about the doggedness of belief or the comforts of autocratic religiosity. Crowd psychologists would have had a field day.

For Catholicism is a fundamentally gregarious and public religion. It's never happy to leave people to private reflections and meditation; perhaps it distrusts their motives or worries about their conclusions. It's uneasy with the querulous promptings of individual logic that may ruin a long-held proof of Church teaching. It has no time for solitary study of the Bible – in which, of course, the word 'Catholic' never appears – preferring that its adherents listen to the teaching and obey without further idle enquiry. (Its concern over the private sinner or worshipper led to the abandoning, in certain parts of the US, of the practice of individual Confession and the arrival of the corporate version, where everyone's sins are undifferentiated and absolution is sought in chorus.)

From the massively generalised Papal Blessing across the world at Easter, down to the exegetical sermon preached by academic Jesuits in outer London parishes over the heads of the snoozing faithful, the Catholic religion delights in bringing people together into communities and smoothing over their essential heterogeneity by insisting on the one-ness of their religious belief.

What are they like, this motley crew that meet to worship God in church together? They're a pretty unprepossessing lot. Unlike the Protestant congregations you see on *Songs of Praise*, Catholics do not sit in serried ranks of sports-jacketed and print-frocked zealotry, singing 'For Those In Peril On the Sea' with tunnel-mouthed conviction and pop-eyed sincerity. Unlike the fashion plates that crowd St Paul's Cathedral or Westminster Abbey for royal weddings, Catholics rarely affect a glamorous exterior. Unlike Evangelicals and Revivalists, they wholly eschew signs of enthusiasm, enjoyment or personal ecstasy.

Instead the local adherents mostly present an aspect of teeth-clenched melancholy, as though they were the inmates of some benign but unforgiving prison camp. They look cowed. They seem badgered. Their silence (although nobody would dream of speaking aloud in church) is the silence of one nagged into submission. They are not having fun.

It was very easy, when young, to feel there was nothing for you there. The worship of God should, it's true, be the main reason and motivation for one's presence at Mass; but since the Church also presents itself as a family and a social meeting-ground, it's only natural to check out one's neighbours and wonder why they're so unendearing. Among the congregation, the old, the sick, the barmy and the terminally decrepit are out in force. Children might clamber on and off the long pews from devil-ment, or run up and down the aisle screaming anarchy ('Wouldn't you think its parents would exercise some discipline,' you could hear the congregation whispering to itself) but of one's putative teenage peer group there was hardly a sign.

Where were the bikers, you asked yourself? Where the parish-hall disco lovelies? Where the Rolling Stones aficionados? Where the boozers from the Fox and Hounds? Where the hell were all the under-twenties? If they wouldn't be seen dead inside a church, what was I doing there? And were the rest of the congregation looking at me at fifteen and seeing, instead of a cool young Terence-Stamp-in-the-making, some prematurely aged neurotic visionary with a guilt complex of Homeric proportions and no friends?

So a sense of alienation grew. From being a devotee (almost entirely because of all the stage-acting that went with being an altar server), I became a sideline spectator, convinced I fitted nowhere in this gathering.

It wasn't difficult to turn a satirical eye on it all. Churches tended to be almost full on Sundays and the sense of community was palpable. The grander families from the slightly superior socio-economic classes inclined heads towards each other, in the accredited Hollywood style of genteel, Sunday-morning religiosity. The full waistcoats of the Legion of Mary lot (greyly middle-aged, bureaucratic and ponderous as police station sergeants) swelled with pride as they drew lots to determine who should take the collection. A brace of ancient female retainers sold copies of *The Universe* and the *Catholic Herald* in the back porch, and acted as a joint clearing-house for the exchange of parish gossip. The whole thing looked like this:

The priest. The servers.

Front row: the readers of the lesson; the good-as-gold Irish lady helpers; the madman.

Prime position: Fecundity Farm. Virtually reserved for husband-and-wife-with-six-children combinations.

Spot the professionals: the doctor and the doctor's wife. The poor accountant with two children (wife Protestant). Given lots of space by respectful locals.

A block vote of over-achieving tradesmen with wives in brown headscarves and winsome children.

The spinsters: ramrod backs, severe goblin faces, stiff curly hair, an atmosphere of genteel desperation.

Sassy girls, unable to get into the choir. Bright colours, absurd hairstyles, coltish demeanour.

The workers: gas fitters, carpet layers, double glazing salesmen.

The blacks: glazed hats, closed eyes, pained faces.

The poor Eastern Europeans: in wool beanie hats and ashen complexions. An atmosphere of overcooked red cabbage hung around them.

The poor Italians: a matronly type in mantilla, and her two grown-up but runtish sons, balding and gawky like twin Neapolitan Stan Laurels.

The Legion of Mary: grey suits, grey faces, red sashes. Terrible singers.

Unaccompanied young mothers with squally babies and an interesting past.

The old Irish: red faces, pioneer badges, best suits for Sunday.

The quick-getaway desperadoes: the smokers. The young London-Irish.

Outside the weekly rituals of Communion, Benediction and Confession, the community rarely met. A local wedding or funeral might inspire a large turnout at someone's home, once the proprieties had been observed at the communal church. A

Queen of the May committee of anxious mothers might meet to discuss where they could lay their hands on cheap taffeta. You might run into the German madwoman in Tesco's, or spot the most earnest of the spinsters haunting the public library. But most of the time, by tacit agreement, the Papists contrived to keep their religious identity off the secular streets.

For some sections of the community, however, the badge of Catholicism counted for more than a set of mere beliefs.

THE IRISH

They, or more specifically, the Irish women, held the parish in thrall. They exercised no power to speak of (the only woman who did was the parish priest's chilly and aloof housekeeper), but their influence was all-pervasive. If the church required an extra sprucing-up, they would advise as to the shade of red paint. If cut flowers were needed for the altar at Easter, they'd forage for blooms down Northcote Road market.

If a new curate felt the least bit uncertain about the effectiveness of his ministry in a tough neighbourhood, he would be sent – discreetly but firmly – round to meet Mrs O'Hara, or the Misses Fogerty, or Mrs Kenneally and her brood. There he would receive a chorus of reassurance as to his wonderful compassion, psychological insight, breadth of wisdom (especially in one so young) and devastating charm. He would also receive a variety of substantial meals (none of the mealy-mouthed Anglican curate's teatime for the Irish matrons; they were used to feeding trenchermen), be invited to join the family for every Church holiday celebration in the foreseeable future, and finally told the door (the back door) would always be open for him.

This unforced generosity towards priests was part of a larger, if perhaps more spurious persona of Irish womanhood – the myth of the near-saint. You could meet a score of such ladies, in varying stages of convincingness, on a single trek round the parish: selflessly good to all, indefatigably kind, constantly on the *qui vive* for opportunities to help the less fortunate. Sweetly nice to all, they could make you feel homicidal. They were so nice and good and unchallengeable. What they were about was obvious: they were walking exponents of every Catholic virtue going. They took themselves, and the idea of the 'perfect' Catholic temperament, very seriously indeed. It was not enough, for them, to keep one's nose clean and lead a blameless life; they had to be seen to be striving for virtue each passing minute.

They also set the moral tempo of the time, tut-tutting with horror about public (especially parliamentary) scandals, patting their hair with tremulous disgust at the news of a local unmarried

pregnancy. They thought John Lennon 'disgusting'. They themselves approved of Val Doonican, but thought his constant guest
Dave Allen flirted with blasphemy too much for comfort. 'Ah
now, we must be charitable', was an almost constant refrain.
Offering to pray for the souls of the misguided, they contrived to
suggest that they'd done everything in their power to help the
fallen of the parish, but really there had to be a limit . . .

THE ROMANTICS

Among the modest numbers of church-going young, the
majority went to Mass solely and simply because their parents
browbeat them into it. The mid-sixties was no time to explore
your teenage relationship with God, any more than it was a time
to start building up a collection of classical records. Genuinely
devoted fifteen-year-olds were a phenomenon (at school they
were generally to be found in the unlovely ranks of the swots and
the pinch-nosed solitaries). But among the callow faithful could
be found a few whose motives were complicated by the fact that
the church was a potentially fruitful ground for romance.

In fact it wasn't at all. Nothing in the eyes from the crabby old
vendors of *The Universe*, or the red-faced church doorman as he
slung back the bolts after the final blessing of the Mass, held any
encouragement to linger in the porch and make dates. But across
the aisles, in the communion queue and in the filing-out
crocodile, by some miracle eyes met surreptitiously and minor
relationships were forged.

The best use that could be made of the local curate was to
engage him in conversation in the street on a Saturday afternoon
and hope that he'd feel like introducing you to any members of
the choir who might be doing their weekend shopping. But how,
once you'd effected an introduction, could you sustain a conver-

sation? With only the electrifying topics of descant-singing and church architecture to bind you together, there was scant hope of it leading anywhere.

THE HOLY FOOLS

A memorable feature of Catholic congregations was that of incipient madness. Every church, indeed every religious movement, draws its fair share of unbalanced converts, desperate for both physical and emotional shelter. But my childhood church-going seemed constantly fretted by the emotionally unstable. I

remember sitting in mortified silence one wintry Saturday as the pleasant, thirtyish lady beside me (I was, I think, nine) drew long shuddering breaths, her eyes tightly shut, as goosepimples rose on the skin of her arms (she wore a short-sleeved blouse although it was freezing). When she opened her eyes, I looked away, only to feel a trembling hand stroke my hair.

I thought of Hansel and the woman from the gingerbread house. I thought of the Snow Queen. I had neither the vocabulary nor the social graces to deal with the situation. My mother, deep in her devotions, noticed nothing until my frozen admirer landed a resounding open-mouthed kiss – more like a bite really – on the side of my head. Quick to action as usual, she hissed, 'Leave the child alone!' and swatted the woman like a wasp. We shifted pews, but nothing was said later. It was par for the course in a church.

I remember the strange man who appeared at Novenas each Saturday, always in an immaculate pink shirt buttoned to the neck but without an accompanying tie. He did nothing to offend the proprieties, beyond walking – gliding – up and down the side aisle, in a slow but deliberate progress, like one stalking a tethered goat. A fixed smile was sealed on to his face like a mask. He had (as Hemingway said of Wyndham Lewis) the eyes of a disappointed rapist. Where did he come from? What did he do? What, more to the point, had he done to provoke these restless, minatory wanderings? As he appeared, distractingly, at different points of the church, before gliding unfussily off to reappear elsewhere, he seemed like a well-turned-out revenant, revisiting some haunted shrine out of grim nostalgia.

At our family's neighbourhood church – a less well-appointed affair, in which the radiators never worked – a German spinster in wire-frame governess spectacles used periodically to storm out of church in mid-sermon, stage-whispering a tirade of criticism. A mutterer and twitterer, she once walloped her umbrella across my father's blameless head because he glanced at her as they passed each other at the baptismal font.

More disconcerting still was a spry, wizened individual with a convict's crew-cut, one Mr Stone, whose descent into madness was accompanied by a certain surreal humour. He would appear at the start of Mass, clad in shorts and singlet and clutching a tennis racquet and a loaf of Mother's Pride, both of which he proudly bore up to receive Holy Communion. His gravelly voice issued from the back row of the congregation, hinting broadly at the parish priest's illicit affairs with various elderly members of his flock. He was excessively fond of Greta Garbo and once, in gratitude for some small kindness my mother had performed, posted through her letter-box a torn-off page of stills from *Ninotchka* showing Garbo in a clinch with John Barrymore. It was said that he had lost his mind when his mother died and embraced religion for the usual reasons – but his condition seemed far more a release from the constraints of social and Catholic protocol than a yielding to them.

THE CATHOLIC PILGRIMAGE

The physical journey as spiritual quest – that was always the symbolic point of the pilgrim's wandering steps. Unfortunately, even before Chaucer pinned his venal Merchants and Reeves and Wives of Bath (all of whom were, of course, devotees of the Old Faith) to the pages of *The Canterbury Tales*, Catholic pilgrims were betraying a disgracefully worldly attitude to the whole idea of a religious Day Out.

Catholic pilgrimages take three distinct forms, according to their destinations. The only elements they all share are their convenors, who tend to be genial, red-faced Salesian Fathers or Christian Brothers, and their tendency to degenerate from listless prayer meetings into mildly wicked adventures among the more worldly and independent.

The Home Counties Pilgrimage

How they resonated through one's ninth and tenth years (the optimum age to get you started on the road to zealotry), those pleasant names of the sites of plaster statue and ding-donging ice-cream van. Walsingham, with its jaunty suggestion of Waltzing Matilda, promised a churchified variant of a bluegrass hoedown, perhaps with a few prayers interspersed between the whoops. Aylesford – a pleasant amalgam of beer and Hay Wain rusticity – in Kent, was a popular destination, a Garden-of-England dream of a town, with the river Medway tinkling by, and country lanes stretching picturesquely in all directions.

The specially hired coach bearing us thirty pilgrims from St Vincent's, Battersea, would wheeze to a halt beside the old pre-Dissolution Friary and disgorge us onto the grass. You could immediately go and say some prayers at one of the modern chapels dedicated to various saints and martyrs, but mostly you'd head for the shrine of St Simon Stock, a rare example of a *man* who once saw an apparition of the Blessed Virgin. Spurning both the local handbook and the local guide, the parish priest would himself give us the lowdown on the beatific Simon, and enjoin us to prayer and good works until it was time for lunch.

It was always supposed to be a picnic lunch, a jolly-good-fun Catholic version of the Anglicans' infamous Sausage Sizzles and Youth Clubs. Invariably, several pilgrims would have failed to pack anything apart from a half bottle of Teachers for the ride home; nobody could afford to go to a posh restaurant; there was no question of waiting for the pot of tea and plate of gateau at 4.15. There was only one solution. Everyone headed for the pub. Some of the more difficult local ladies would determinedly stay outside in the car park with us whingeing pre-adolescents (sated on sherbert fountains and Jubbly triangles of iced orange juice) rather than sully themselves by going in. The men would try to persuade them that it was really more 'an hotel lounge' than a boozer, but unavailingly. The afternoons would be spent in small recriminations, smaller flirtations, a few prayers and some companionable little walks by the greyish stream of the Medway. The overriding feeling was one of complete pointlessness.

The Irish Pilgrimage

There's no gentility about Irish pilgrimages. They tend to be grim affairs full of self-mortification and pain. The Irish are never content merely to admire their saints and martyrs and visionaries; they try to emulate them in their suffering, to give themselves as hard a time as possible in order to 'offer it up' for the souls of the Faithful Departed or receive merit points from an impressed celestial jury.

The most famous shrine in Ireland is the eccentrically named Knock in Co. Mayo, on the Atlantic seaboard, where the Virgin Mary appeared to some villagers at the turn of the century. It now has its own airport, thanks to the local Monsignor Horan's persuasive way with the Prime Minister Charles Haughey when he was seeking the support of the Mayo voters in the run-up to an election. But it's perceived as a kind of low-rent version of Lourdes, with all the souvenir tat but without the attendant glamour. For the real flavour of masochistic Irish pilgrimage you have to turn to two considerably wilder venues: The Reek and Lough Derg.

The Reek is the colloquial name given to Croagh Patrick, a forbidding mountain near Westport (again in Mayo) on the Atlantic seaboard. Irish men and women converge on it in great numbers on the last Sunday in July. Its three-and-a-half-mile incline isn't steep, but is full of flinty stones. The foothills are boggy, and arriving pilgrims must wear heavy boots along with their rucksack of sandwiches, Thermos and fruit. Half a mile from the top, just when you're feeling that this punishing SAS-style endurance test has gone on long enough, the Stations of the Cross begin. At the top is an altar, where a priest officiates constantly throughout the day; as soon as you begin your agonising climb, you're deemed to be at Mass. When you arrive at the summit plateau, you must remove your shoes and socks or tights and circumvent the altar seven times. Some people choose to drag themselves round the whole painful course on their knees, saying the Rosary.

For the last word in righteous suffering, though, nothing beats Lough Derg. What goes on there is known as St Patrick's Purgatory. A very strict timetable monitors your every move. You have to fast for three days. You rise at 7 a.m., and head for Donegal where a small boat ferries you across to the island (Lough Derg means the Red Lake). There you remove shoes and socks and walk about the bleak and punishing terrain until 3 p.m. when you're allowed a slice of dry bread, of the consistency of concrete, and a teabag floating in a mug of hot red lakewater. Anyone thinking to ask for milk and sugar will be scoffed at.

Everyone then sits up all night, saying the Rosary and listening to sermons until 7 a.m. Still without sleep or the basic comforts, you hear Mass, do the Stations of the Cross and walk the lacerating stones until 8 p.m., when you're finally allowed to go to bed. Next day you leave the island at midday (invariably singing 'Hail Glorious St Patrick, Dear Saint of Our Isle') and go home – but you're still fasting, so the smell (as my mother remembers it) of boiling gammon and scallions drives you away. You're not allowed anything to eat till two the following morning, should you happen to still be alive.

Why do they do it? Because whatever you want, whatever

spiritual reward you may desire, will unconditionally be yours if you do. It's like the final test from some dark medieval rite, some harrowing life-and-death challenge from the Dark Ages. People still go off to it, every year.

The Lourdes Pilgrimage

Nobody who goes to Lourdes forgets the experience easily. The combination of group emotion, of everyone's palpable devotion to something unseen, the simplicity and grandeur of 'the Domain', the feeling that – as you move from your pleasant hotel, with its chit-chat and litre flagons of local beer, strapping on your black armband to signify your readiness to be a stretcher-bearing *brancardier* or helper of the stricken into the baths – you're occupying some curious entrepot between life and death . . . well, it's all calculated to shake up the most cynical spirit. The underbelly of Lourdes – the extreme stupidity, greed, opportunism, smugness, hypocrisy and vapid credulity – makes its presence felt too at intervals, but generally it's damped down by a shared commitment to belief and to getting healed in body or soul.

The Lourdes legend has been around for 130 years. It was 1858 when a bright but uneducated millworker's daughter of fourteen called Bernadette Soubirous went gathering sticks and saw, in a nearby rose bush, an apparition of a beautiful woman in white, beckoning to her. On a second occasion, the entranced Bernadette knelt immobile and staring, and had to be physically carried back to her home.

Thereafter she saw what she took to be the Virgin Mary a further eleven times, each visit being accompanied by an ever-increasing throng of local spectators. Bernadette was ticked off by the local priest, slapped by her parents, disbelieved by the chief of police and grilled by the town prosecutor, but never altered her story. A groundswell of popular enthusiasm had taken firm charge of the 'apparition' story by the time Bernadette left the district. Local devotees and out-of-town believers came to leave money and statues and petitions in little envelopes. Even before the innocent visionary had gone, the first seller of souvenirs had turned up.

By the 1960s, the tacky, plastic-souvenir side of Lourdes had become an ancient cliché. The more fatuous of the local Clapham ladies who went every year still returned triumphantly clutching their plastic sheep with nodding heads (Bernadette was a shepherdess), their flashing plastic grottoes, their miniature TV sets containing images of the apparitions (as though helpfully translating them into the iconographic currency of the media age), their moulded-plastic statues of the Virgin Mary surmounted by a halo bearing the inscription *Je suis l'Immaculate Conception*', the blue plastic bottles of Lourdes Water again moulded into the Virgin's shape, but with an unscrewable head . . .

Certainly you could still get all these indispensable items ten years ago, whether at Tarbes airport or the narrow streets that led like spokes away from the hub of the Domain. But they no longer seemed offensively materialistic intrusions of the oafish outside world upon the devotions of the transcendent. No one minded them any more. They were looked on with a kindly indulgence, like some backward or wayward child. Why? Because there was a new Catholic spirit in the air. Its watchword was not censorship, nor restraint, nor earnestness, but joy. It was part of a new, rather unappealing kind of Christianity, full of clear-eyed blandness and ersatz ecstasy among the believers.

CATHOLIC INS AND OUTS

Out	*In*
Vinegarised altar Valpolicella	Paul Masson altar Zinfandel
400-page leatherette missals	Four-page missalettes
The Catholic Women's League	Female deacons (who can hand out Communion)
Choirs	Folk-rock combo with cheerleaders
Plaster statues	Wall-hangings in velour and chenille
Unleavened communion hosts	Wheatgerm communion hosts
Hellfire sermons	Folksy chats à la Rabbi Blue
Fasting	Greed
St Christopher	Lech Walesa

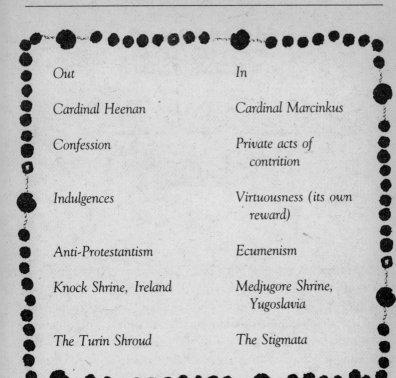

Out	In
Cardinal Heenan	Cardinal Marcinkus
Confession	Private acts of contrition
Indulgences	Virtuousness (its own reward)
Anti-Protestantism	Ecumenism
Knock Shrine, Ireland	Medjugore Shrine, Yugoslavia
The Turin Shroud	The Stigmata

Epilogue

Going Off The Idea

IT HAPPENS QUITE SIMPLY. One day, in church, in Confession or simply walking down the street, you start to lose your faith. For some people, they find they have sat looking for too long at that curtained little house on the altar, inside which reposes the central image of their religious beliefs – the sacramental Host – and decide that they have looked upon nothingness once too often.

For others, it's tied inextricably to sex. Having discovered something overwhelming, satisfying and intensely good – a necessary part of their new sense of relationships – they can no longer stand to be told it's wrong, in Confession after Confession. For one thing it's embarrassing, for another it's simply tiresome. So they stop going. A residual sense of guilt, which will itself take years to shake off, tells them they cannot take Communion, nor indeed attend Mass while in a state of (now only supposed) mortal sin, leads them to abandon the second most crucial of the regular sacraments. And gradually the whole tapestry of belief becomes unwoven.

━━━━━━━━━━━━━━━ JO FOLEY ━━━━━━━━━━━━━━━

I stopped being religious when I first discovered sex. Once I'd
done it, I knew I couldn't go back to the church because I knew
I'd want to do it again. I got married in a Catholic church
because to do otherwise would have upset my mother. Later, I
had a chat with a very nice old priest who said that sometimes,
if a marriage was not enriched by having children, then they're
not that important. But from that day to this I have been afraid
of living in mortal sin. I found I just couldn't take the priest's
word for it. Not after twenty years of believing something else.

For me it was the confessional. At fourteen or fifteen, I was
becoming (I admit) an intellectual snob. I pooh-poohed the idea
that any external authority could decide what was or wasn't good
for me to read, see or think if I chose to. I was too bolshy to
believe any longer that disobedience was a sin; it became a series
of revolutionary postures. I decided that missing Mass, telling
strategic untruths, having fantasies about the Angelas and Kates
that populated the adolescent world, were only sins if I inwardly
judged them to be so. I still believed in God, and Jesus and
Salvation. Why should anyone else decide for me which forms
my conscience should take?

━━━━━━━━━━━━━━━ MARY CRAIG ━━━━━━━━━━━━━━━

I left my convent at seventeen with inhibitions impenetrable, a
deep fear of life, an armoury of draconian laws to govern my
every action, and no sense at all of a loving God. It was only
because I dared not do otherwise that I continued to call myself
a Catholic.

My parents noticed this turn in my behaviour with their usual concerned sympathy, but (as Catholic parents always will) attributed it to a dozen irrelevant causes. They blamed the company I kept, the onslaughts of the permissive society, the influence of John Lennon – and they tried to do something about it. When the local curate came round for his usual nightcap, after a short period of chat my father would remember something of burning importance down in the surgery, and my mother would disappear for half an hour to make tea. The hapless cleric, duly briefed, would enquire why I had ceased attending the sacraments and whether there was anything 'worrying' me. I would argue and complain in a tone of high (but secular) moral rigour; he would be all smiles and reassurance, and encourage me to pray to ward off such alarming fancies. What he would never do was appreciate that I was in the glorious throes of liberation and never considered my doubts an affliction at all.

Years have gone by, and my faith has rocked back and forth, through trips to Lourdes, periods of blank atheism and denunci- ation, querulous agnosticism, and sudden returns to the fold. I still go to church, more for social reasons than any other, and always feel obscurely comforted by doing so. But Catholicism, for me as for thousands, has turned into a racial identity. As much as any lapsed Buddhist, Jew or Muslim, the grown-up Catholic feels a constant pull towards his or her roots that has nothing to do with the current intensity of their faith. It manifests itself thus:

Sins of omission: the constant sense of failing to do something that is required of you, something better, more morally correct, more pleasing to God than whatever you're doing now.

The Sign of the Cross: finding that you cannot pass a Catholic church (the others don't count) or a funeral procession without tugging a metaphorical forelock; making the old, old sign quite involuntarily just as the plane is about to take off for the Far East.

The sense of sacrilege: finding you can still be appalled to see a Rosary treated as a fashion accessory, whether by Madonna, the *Tatler* or a couture victim in South Molton Street.

Discipline: thinking that the strictures of the present, hard-line Pope may be logically reprehensible but that, in their affirmation of what's infallibly right and true, they offer a better direction to the Catholic flock than the bland compromises of the Church of England.

Saints: discovering yourself making a bitten-back plea to St Anthony to locate a crucial document that has gone missing.

Key dates: it is still unthinkable that one could pass Christmas or Easter without going to church, passionately devoted to a ritual that no longer holds the same transcendent meaning for you.

CLARE TOYNBEE

My sisters and I were all plagued by guilt. I feel guilty about almost *everything*. I spend my life trying to make people not criticise me. I still expect criticism, but now I want them to do it to my face.

When I left the Church I thought I'd left it for good. The only thing that brought me back was to go and light a candle for my child who had died. I did the same four years running, on the anniversary. I just needed that small ritual.

Most of all, you're left with a residue of guilt. Years of self-examination for signs of sin (real or imagined) are not to be sloughed off so easily. It now manifests itself as a feeling that you're always about to be blamed for something, and that when you are you will have no defence, because in the judgment of the Lord (who is of course infinitely just, beyond human understanding) you're always in the wrong. At home, at work, in relationships, in arguments, some nagging sense of wrong-doing trips you up. It is a disabling hangover from those early years, perhaps the thing that leaves you most embittered about your Catholic past.

Many things, on the other hand, remain attractive in hindsight: the sense of belonging to a global, indeed galactic, community; the inner warmth that fuelled the mundane heart as you stood in a cold Battersea kitchen before hurrying out to seven a.m. Mass during Lent; the shriving of all guilts and fears that followed Saturday visits to Confession; the intellectual stimulation of arguing tiny points of doctrine with Jesuit fathers, when your faith was grounded in foundations of concrete.

Most of all, you miss the certainties that went with Catholicism. It is possible to feel envy for older Catholics – my mother and her friends, for instance – for whom no earthly problem or crisis does not find its solution through applying to the agony column of the Catechism, the advice bureaux of the priests, nuns and popes; and, especially, of each other.

For the lapsed, the world suddenly reverts to being a chilly, uncertain, contingent place in which you are a random digit rather than a potentially blessed primary number. Remembering what you have lost – indeed fought to lose – after all those years with the difficult, absorbing, threatening but finally heartening data of religious induction, you know with a heavy certainty that what they told you at seven is true: you may leave the Catholic Church with a high, exhausted and relieved heart; but somehow, to the end of your life, it will never leave you.